Divers Information *on the* Romantic History *of*

St. CROIX

Containing much information of value to the Reader about Whim Greathouse *&* Old Plantation Days; the Story of Sugar & Rum; *description of Life on a Cruzan Plantation; the story of the* Sugar Cane Plant; Alexander Hamilton's *account of a terrible Hurricane; & the story of our famous Governor,* Peter von Scholten. *Also the connection between* Rum and the American Revolution.

By Florence Lewisohn

Fourth Printing
Published by The St. Croix Landmarks Society
Copyright 1964 by Florence Lewisohn
Library of Congress Card No. 65-11869
Printed by Dukane Press, Inc.

Book Design by Ralph Bell Fuller

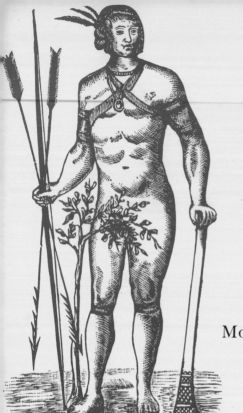

CARIB WARRIOR

C. E. Taylor woodcut from LeClerc

CONTENTS ✠ PAGE

HIGHLIGHTS OF CRUZAN HISTORY

ST. CROIX today is an hospitable island that has a little of everything except cold weather.

The island has changed remarkably since Columbus discovered it in 1493 and was driven off by hostile Indians. In the nearly 500 years that have intervened, this little area of 84 square miles and 52,628 acres has alternately suffered and prospered from the blind forces of nature and history. It has attracted a remarkable variety of people during its history, not all of whom benefited the island.

During the period of development of the Western Hemisphere, St. Croix was fought over, colonized, bought, sold, captured and recaptured because of its strategic or economic potential. It is popularly said to have existed under the flags of seven nations. This tally does not include periods of possession or use by aboriginal tribes, pirates, filibusters, squatters, private owners, religious and trading companies, or the few times when it was not occupied by anyone at all.

Our documented history begins with the Indians found on the island by Columbus, and seen again by Governor John White 94 years later when he stopped here three days on his way to found Virginia in 1587.

THE VANISHED INDIAN. When Columbus sent his men ashore at St. Croix's Salt River entrance to look for fresh water, November 14, 1493, the landing party encountered a canoe full of Indians and a lively fight took place on the water. Columbus' men got more or less the worst of it, but captured a few Indians whom they took with them. Columbus named the spot "Cabo de Flechas" or "Cape of The Arrows."

When the island came to be actually settled in the early 1600's, there were no Indians left. It is assumed that most of them were carried off in raids by the Spaniards to work the gold mines of Santo Domingo.

To this day the question re-

INDIAN CANOE

3

mains unsettled as to whether St. Croix was inhabited by the warlike, cannibalistic Caribs or the peaceful Arawaks, or both. The Arawak culture predominated, as artifacts show, but the cultural traits were carried by the women, and the Caribs as they moved northward through the Antilles from the Orinoco area, liked nothing better than capturing Arawak women. There is also evidence of strong relationships with the warlike Tainans of Puerto Rico, and the peaceful Taino of Hispaniola, who sometimes had women as chieftains.

In any case, St. Croix has at least forty Indian village sites, and is rich in Indian artifacts.* The Salt River village site is a favorite digging spot for local amateurs.

An archaeologist once uncovered a row of flat stone slabs standing on edge at Salt River, with petroglyphs and pictographs on them. Hundreds of the "three pointer" religious stones were found there, and are still to be picked up along the shore or inland. The still-visible earthen fort built there by the French in the 1650's abounds in shell deposits and other Indian artifacts. There are also sites at Estates St. George, Fair Plain, Glynn, Grove Place, Plessen, Coakley Bay, Cane Bay, Longford and Sprat Hall, to mention just a few.

1493 **SPAIN.** Columbus discovered St. Croix and named it Santa Cruz (Holy Cross) on his second voyage. The Indians called it "Ay Ay"; spelled also as "Iahi" or "Agay" by early writers.

1587 **ENGLAND.** John White, sent by Sir Walter Raleigh as Governor of Virginia, stayed here three days; found evidence of Indian habitation.

1625 **HOLLAND & ENGLAND.** Both nations began small settlements; Dutch near Bassin; English on SW shore area. French filibusters had been using island as base for careening boats for years.

1642 Holland increased its settlement, called it Nieuw Zeeland, later Nieuw Walcheron. Still held jointly with the English, but under much dissension. Tobacco and indigo chief products. English had an early sugar works.

DOUBLE DEALINGS BY THE DUTCH, ENGLISH & FRENCH. The story of these settlements on St. Croix is a cloak and dagger one with its details lost in history. The historian John Knox reasons that the Dutch preceded the English by a few years, but it is certain that both were there by 1625. The Dutch and a few

*The Folmer Andersen Collection given to the National Park Service in Christiansted by the former St. Croix Museum.

4

hundred French Huguenots from St. Kitts lived in or near Bassin, while the English settled on the south shore not far from present-day Frederiksted.

Affairs muddled along until 1645. By then the colonies had a good high tone with a Dutch Governor-General appointed by their West India Company, and some English noblemen with letters-patent from the King. By that year there were some 600 persons on the island.

Then things came to a boil. That year the Dutch Governor killed the English one in his house, and a rousing fight took place between the two colonies, with the Dutch Governor wounded and dying a few days later. The Dutch chose another Governor and he was asked to visit the English, who promised him protection. This promise was violated; he was seized, condemned and publicly shot. The Dutch, being the weaker, decided to abandon their colony and left for St. Eustatius and St. Martins. The French, who had sympathized with the Dutch, asked permission to leave. They were sent off to Guadaloupe in an English ship after they promised to give the captain their abandoned plantations.

When they arrived at Guadaloupe, the refugees registered protests against the captain. He was seized, imprisoned and his ship and cargo sold. "All this," says Knox, "made quite a noise in England, France and the Islands."

646 **ENGLAND** held island after Dutch & French driven out.

650 **SPAIN.** Duke of Marlborough's English settlement massacred or driven out by 1,200 Spaniards from Puerto Rico. Many went to Bermuda. The Dutch from St. Eustatius tried to recapture it the same year; defeated by the Spanish Garrison.

650 **FRANCE.** Governor de Poincy of other French West Indies took possession for French crown; planned to make it his capitol.

651 **DE POINCY** bought St. Croix and other islands from French King, for private domain. As a leading Knight of Malta, he sent other Knights and Frenchmen to colonize St. Croix.

Mavon du gouverneur

DU BOIS' PALACE at JUDITH'S FANCY

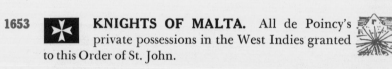

1653 ✠ **KNIGHTS OF MALTA.** All de Poincy's private possessions in the West Indies granted to this Order of St. John.

1657 Chevalier de la Mothe sent by de Poincy with supplies for relief of inhabitants. Some 200 rebellious French colonists put de Mothe in chains and sailed off in his ship, presumably to Brazil. Two years later, the new Governor, Chevalier du Bois, sent to restore order.

THE DAYS OF THE FRENCH. Sieur du Bois built a "castle" in 1659 on Hemer's Peninsula which is now Estate Judith's Fancy. The ruins of this residence stand today, done in the old French style of a small chateau, with two unusual towers at either end, one of which is still there. Legend has it that du Bois brought in our small white tailed deer to the island to stock his estate park with them.

The French government headquarters lay along the east bank of Salt River, which then was a real river arising near Canaan and coming down through Estate Concordia into the Salt River Bay.

On the opposite bank of the bay, the Knights of Malta threw up a triangular earthenwork, called *Fort Sàle*. Its outline is still visible today if one scrambles through the underbrush to find it. Upriver from the Fort just off the present-day Northshore road was the French landing stage and customs house. This site was later used by the Danes as a guardpoint. Somewhere above on the present Kirkegaard Hill was the Jacobin, or Dominican monastery shown on old French maps. It was here that Père Labat, the famous writer-priest is believed to have once stayed on one of his many journeys between French islands.

The French had a fairly difficult time on St. Croix. The Knights were aristocrats and not used to the hard work of running plantations. There were six-hundred men among them who could bear arms, but not too many who understood the problems of running a sugar, indigo or tobacco plantation, all of which they attempted.

It was these Frenchmen who at one time burned off all they could of St. Croix's dense forests and lived on their ships until the fires ceased. They wanted more land for cultivating, and believed that the forests caused their strange fevers, and night vapours.

By 1671, the French had built another Fort or Battery at Bassin, the present-day

6

Christiansted. It stood on the point at the entrance to the harbor, and was called *Fort Saint Jean.* Later the Danes rebuilt it and renamed it Fort Louise Augusta.

The Knights of Malta gave up on St. Croix, but the name they gave the island stayed with it, if not their pronunciation.

Judith — whose Fancy the old du Bois estate became — was Judith A. Letta Benners, born Heyliger in 1762. Her tombstone may be seen today near the old Castle-Greathouse ruins. Back of the ruin stand some Danish additions — a windmill and the later-period chimney from steammill days, with the sugar factory ruins nearby.

1665 **FRENCH WEST INDIA COMPANY** bought St. Croix and all the other islands held by Knights of Malta.

1674 **FRANCE.** King paid off Company debts and took possession.

1695 **ABANDONED.** French King ordered all inhabitants removed to Santo Domingo. France still claimed it but island was not officially settled. Sometimes it was uninhabited; ships of all nations used harbor. English planned a settlement in 1720, but did not carry it out. French renewed their claim in 1727 by taking seven English merchant vessels in the harbor. An undetermined number of English families were squatters there, and remained under the Danes.

1733 **DANISH WEST INDIA AND GUINEA COMPANY** bought St. Croix from the French Crown.

1755 **DENMARK** took over the island as a Crown Colony.

THE DAYS OF THE DANES. The first colonization of St. Croix under Denmark came in 1734, when a few Moravian missionaries cleared six estates given them by the Danish Chamberlain de Pless . . . they found the British families raising cane and making rum when they arrived. The next year, the West India and Guinea Company began to survey the island

7

and to divide it into 150 and 300 acre plantations, as well as into nine quarters! To encourage settlement, land costs were extremely low, and some tax benefits were offered. The planters flocked in from St. Thomas, Tortola, Virgin Gorda, Montserrat and other islands. Soon there were five English estates to every one held by a Dane. Things did not go too well however, and 1753 found the settlers petitioning the Danish King to make St. Croix a Crown Colony as the Company was almost bankrupt. This was accomplished by sale at about one and one-half million dollars. The settlement flourished with a population of over 10,000 by 1755, and some 375 plantations under cultivation with sugar, cotton, indigo and tobacco as main crops.

During the following half century St. Croix's economy, based on sugar and rum and the slave trade, rose steadily to a phenomenal peak. The first event to disturb this picture was the protracted quarrel over slavery which went on between the planters on St. Croix and the more liberal government in Denmark. This same problem confronted every European nation which had colonies in the West Indies or trading stations in Africa. In St. Croix it culminated in:

1792 The Danish Government declared the slave trade to be unlawful, but helped planters to buy slaves during a transition period.

1795-1800 These years marked the peak of prosperity and of the sugar and rum economy; planters foresaw the beginning of the end.

1801 St. Croix captured by the British; restored to Denmark in a few months.

1803 The slave trade was completely abolished by Denmark.

1807-1815 Taken and held by British during Napoleonic Wars. The English planters, who had complained of stiff Danish trade restrictions and limited markets

ESTATE SHOYS

Courtesy "Vore
Gamle Tropekolonier"

were not dissatisfied. The island, however, was returned to Denmark. During the next 30 years, the island's economy worsened with droughts, political upheavals and wars in Europe, and a general depression.

1848 Governor von Scholten freed the slaves on St. Croix, after rioting began.

1866 A disastrous fire in Christiansted in February.

1867 Earthquake and tidal wave. Further decline in economy.

1871 Capitol moved from St. Croix to St. Thomas.

1872 Severe hurricane destroyed crops and buildings.

1875 The Danish government lent the island money to build a Central Sugar Factory, and construction began the next year.

1876 A severe hurricane; followed by depression years until about 1888.

1878-1892 Serious labor riots took place in 1878 and Fredericksted was partially burned. Later the Capitol was divided, with the Governor to reside six months in St. Croix and six in St. Thomas each year. Financial difficulties came through valueless Mexican silver; this silver was abandoned, causing local riots in 1892. The island's economy was at a low ebb.

1917 **THE UNITED STATES.** When the United States bought the three islands in 1917, mainly to keep them out of the hands of the Germans during the First World War, hopes rose high in St. Croix for better days ahead; hopes that were not fulfilled for some years. The island became first a possession under U.S. Navy administration, a period which was satisfactory to no one. As the economy

POCKET ALMANAC for 1863   Courtesy Toby Schoyer

Estate's Name.	Owner's Name.	S M Steam Mill. W M Wind Mill.	Domestic Servants.	Fishermen.	Tradesmen.	Field laborers & pasture people.			Laborers not engaged to work in the field.			Stock belonging to the Estate.							Cultivation.	
						1st class.	2d class.	3d class.	1st class.	2d class.	3d class.	Horses or ponies	Mules.	Asses	Horned Cattle. Calves included.	Sheep.	Goats.	Hogs.	Acres of land in cane and fallow	Total number of acres.
Carlton	W Peebles	SM	6	5	1	55	20	19	0	0	0	4	16	2	124	0	0	0	324	594
Whim	H Knight	WM	7	1	0	25	15	5	3	0	0	0	0	0	45	0	0	0	110	150
Camporico	Messrs. Lang	WM	7	2	3	40	12	15	0	0	0	1	14	0	34	0	0	0	160	500
Hannahsrest	W Beech	....	9	0	0	7	9	2	0	0	0	0	0	0	11	0	8	0	67	200
Stoneyground	J Y Stevens	....	11	0	0	6	3	4	0	0	0	0	0	0	15	0	0	0	0	155
Whitesbay	A Stevenson	....	0	0	0	8	1	1	0	0	0	0	0	0	6	34	0	0	0	91

began a gradual slow rise, it was dashed again by the impact of Prohibition on the rum industry. Later, toward the end of the depression years, the U.S. Congress gave the island its Territorial Organic Act or Constitution, which defined its relationship to the U.S. under the Department of The Interior, with an appointed Governor and an elected local Senate. St. Croix continued to muddle along with an uneven economy until the mid-1950's when the influx of tourists began. Since then there has been a steady growth, based on the island's re-discovery, by those seeking retirement, new business enterprise and investment, or just a lovely tropical vacation.

HARVESTING CANE

GATHERING THE CANE.

THE SUGAR CANE PLANT

(Saccharum Officinarum)

DURING all these centuries and changes of ownership; during years of flux and change, of economic ups and downs in a variable world, one thing remained constant on St. Croix: the importance of sugar cane.

Some English families are thought to have brought in the first cuttings of sugar cane. The French put it into extensive cultivation here in the early 1650's, along with indigo and tobacco.

It was the importance of sugar cane that led to the Danish purchase of St. Croix and the years of the island's greatest prosperity in the late 1700's.

Today we see the relics of this affluent era in the shells of old windmills which appear everywhere, plus the picturesque ruins of sugar factories, rum distilleries and Greathouses which dot the island.

The history of St. Croix, the West Indies and the world would have been quite different without the sugar cane plant, once described as "more valuable than the gold of Peru."

ONE OF THE WORLD'S MOST FAMOUS TRAVELLERS.

Sugar cane, long thought to have originated in Asia, has been proved by recent botanical investigations to have made its start on the island of New Guinea. From there it spread in prehistoric times to much of southeast Asia and to some of the Pacific islands.

One of the earliest mentions of cane juice is in the Buddha legends of the fourth century B.C. One of the original names for white sugar was the Persian word *kandi* from which comes our word candy. The East Indian word

11

shakar or *sheker* is the origin of our word sugar. The ancient botanical name was also corrupted into *Zuccharum* and *Zucra*. The Spanish called it *Azucar* and the English called it Sugar.

The Old Testament twice mentions the cane as a trade article and some Biblical tribes are thought to have understood the art of granulation by evaporation.

It was grown in the Eastern Mediterranean and when the Arabs burst forth they carried it with them to Spain where there was a flourishing sugar industry before the year 1000.

Christian soldiers enjoyed the juice when in the Holy Land during the Crusades. They found sugar cane growing at Acra, Tripoli, and on the islands of Rhodes and Malta. In 1166, the second King of Sicily gave the monastery of St. Bennet a sugar cane grinding mill.

Cane reached Madeira in 1420 and the Azores, Canaries and West Africa shortly afterward. Another of its early voyages was to the island of Madagascar probably from somewhere in Indonesia.

The cane variety which was brought to the Mediterranean was carried by Columbus to Hispaniola on his second voyage. It is reported that this first shipment was lost, but in any case, cane was being grown there in 1507 and the first sugar was made there in 1509. From Hispaniola the sugar cane soon reached Cuba, Puerto Rico and some of the other West Indies, as well as Mexico in 1520, Peru in 1533 and Brazil in 1552. This cane variety, still grown in India under the name of *puri* was very sweet and easy to mill, but gave very low yields and was subject to disease.

Many of the early historians and writers asserted that wild sugar cane was already growing in Mexico, Hispaniola, Brazil and along the Mississippi. It is true that there was plenty of "cane" in the New World, but it wasn't sugar cane, and the early historians and adventurers were easily and quite frequently confused about this.

Captain Cook outdistanced all the other claimants — he found true sugar cane growing on some of the islands of the Pacific Ocean. It is supposed that some Polynesians came from New Guinea or near it and brought sugar cane with them to other islands.

In this hemisphere, it was the Spanish in Hispaniola and the Dutch and Portuguese in Brazil who first made good use of the cane. As early as 1535, the Spanish had some thirty animal mills grinding it on Hispaniola. The first mill in Puerto Rico was in 1524.

We are indebted to the Dutch for introducing sugar cane to the lower part of the West Indies along with their "secrets" of sugar making. They set up their own West India Company in Holland in 1621 and, as merchants for the islands, ranged from lower Brazil to the North American colonies in their own ships. They learned sugar making in Brazil and when the Dutch Jews there were driven out by 1626 they moved northward and helped to found the sugar industry in the French and British West Indies. They brought in cane cuttings and taught the planters all they knew, supplying them with equipment from Europe on credit against their first crop.

A Dutchman brought the first cuttings to Barbados in 1637, but it wasn't until five years later that a Dutch merchant there supplied rollers, coppers for boiling and other equipment on credit for a factory. A plantation began on Martinique in 1639, and on nearby Guadaloupe, Governor Houel had a flourishing sugar factory going with Dutch help by 1647.

All the Dutch were ejected from Brazil by 1654 and were scattered on every West Indian island as bankers, merchants, advisors and traders. Their style of windmill dotted hilltops on every island. By the 1660's the French, again with Dutch help, began to refine white sugar in a new "claying" process. The English and other nationalities made wet brown muscavado sugar with now and then a little "clayed" or "plantation white" for their own use.

Meanwhile, sugar cane was travelling down from Hispaniola and Puerto Rico through the islands in this area. It is not known from where or when the first sugar cane reached St. Croix. Old records indicate an "Englishman's Sugar Works" on the south shore, perhaps around 1625.

In 1657, the French were temporarily driven out of Madagascar and carried with them the cane varieties they found growing there, which

Courtesy New York Public Library

CULTIVATING CANE

13

were different from the one brought by Columbus. They planted them first on the island of Reunion, then known as Bourbon, and later the varieties were moved to Mauritius in 1715 and from there the French carried them to their Pacific Colony of Tahiti. One variety did so well it was taken to the French West Indian islands, and under the name of "Otaheite" or Bourbon or simply White Cane, soon displaced almost all of the original varieties.

The Danes were the last of the European powers to get in on the sugar treasure when they acquired the Virgin Islands. By 1800 here, the Otaheite cane was *the* cane of St. Croix and the other Caribbean islands. Like its predecessor, the Otaheite went down in the West Indies with a new disease about 1875, but fortunately the possibility of producing new varieties by breeding had been discovered in Barbados in 1858, and "rediscovered" about 1888 in both Barbados and Java.

New cane varieties, ever higher yielding and resistant to each new disease and parasite have come forth in enormous numbers in later years.

The sugar canes now grown on St. Croix, for example, can produce five times as much sugar per acre as the best cane grown when the windmill was built at Whim.
ON GROWING CANE. The cane plant "ratoons" or renews itself for varying numbers of years. In St. Croix, it was customary to replant new cuttings every five or six years, in newly-hoed and manured furrows three or four feet apart. Some fields needed to be replanted every two or three years.

In our area, St. Kitts had the reputation of growing the best cane during the good years — the cane "that answers so well in the pan" with the most sugar in the juice. Yield also varied from year to year with the weather, soil and cultivation. Early planters enriched their soil with such things as coal, vegetable ashes from the sugar boilers, white lime, cane trash of decayed leaves and stems, dung and grass from the cattle pens, the good mould from "guts" and other waste material.

The job of making new furrows, manuring, setting in the new cuttings, etc. was so arduous that it took all available labor each year to replant new acreage.

It took the cane from 14 to 16 months to ripen for cutting. The average juice extracted contained eight parts of pure water to one of sugar, and close to one part of starch, dextrin, protein, wax and other colloidal matter. Some juice was so rich as to make a hogshead of sugar (1,600 lbs.) from 1,300 gallons of juice, and some so poor as to require twice that amount to make a hogshead. Planters reckoned a good recovery if they got a pound of raw sugar from a gallon of raw juice.

CHRISTIANSTED from ESTATE BULOW'S MINDE   Courtesy "Vore Gamle Tropekolonier"

THE AGE OF OPULENCE

ST. CROIX, slow to start, became the richest sugar island in the Caribbean for a time. Under the ownership of Denmark, it reached its peak of wealth and opulence about 1796 when it had 114 windmills and 144 animal or ox mills grinding out the golden juice – which by some West Indian magic turned quickly to gold.

Plantation life is usually thought of in the rosy, romanticised terms of the rich sugar planter lolling at his ease in a luxurious mansion, while myriads of Negroes toiled his fields and ground his cane in contented bondage. This picture is almost a myth as history proves — but not quite — for in the heyday of sugar and rum, it did look like this from the surface.

The planters worked hard to establish their estates and to maintain them, for it took a substantial investment and careful supervision to get started. The planters made money when the sugar and rum markets were up, and some did live in splendor equal to the upper classes of Europe. They built impressive mansions, often copied from their favorite European styles, filled with fine furniture, china, silver and all the appurtenances of wealth. They rode in elegant carriages drawn by fine

15

horses. Some of the more flamboyant planters vied with each other in giving elaborate balls and other amusements, with the customary emphasis on vintage wines and rich food. There were brilliant official government functions. Children were sent to Denmark, France, England or Holland to school.

The usual plantation consisted of an owner's Greathouse, a manager's house, a workers' "village" and many factory buildings where the sugar and rum were made after the windmill ground the cane. The time of "crop" in the Spring, when the cane was cut was a time of feverish day and night activity; with the slaves working in shifts around the clock.

When "crop" was over, the raw or muscavado sugar was off on the high seas for Europe, and the rum-still was going strong to utilize the molasses residue. Rum often meant the difference between profit and loss. After the sugar-making, the plantation settled back again into its months of normalcy, with fields to be tended or replanted, tools and equipment to be repaired at the smithy where huge eight-foot bellows were manned by hand. The wheelwright was busy with wagon repairs, the cooper worked on new hogsheads and rum puncheons for the next crop.

One of the problems of a plantation was that each planter had to own enough slaves to be certain of labor at crop time, while the rest of the year they sometimes became an ill-afforded luxury. For this reason, the Negroes planted, hoed, manured and weeded cane by hand in the West Indies long after the time when other sugar areas of the world were using the plough. Windmills and animal mills persisted in some of the West Indies also long after steammills were available. St. Croix replaced these windmills with steam earlier than did the other islands — the first steammill was at Estate Hogansborg in 1816, at Whim and others in the 1830's.

Island visitors are always intrigued with the fanciful names given to the old St. Croix estates. They have a quality of poetry or a hint of hidden meaning in them. There were Humbug, Bulow's Minde, Retreat, Tipperary, Barren Spot, Judith's and Mary's and Sally's Fancy, Upper Love and Lower Love, Work and Rest, Wheel of Fortune, Hard Labor, and Slob — which despite its name once sold for about $70,000 for 400 acres of cane. There were Hope and Blessing, Envy and Jealousy, Parasol and Paradise, Rust op Twist (Dutch for Rest After Strife,

Struggle or Toil), Solitude and Sweet Bottom, Bog of Allan and Mt. Misery, Northstar and Morningstar, Jerusalem and Sion Hill, Punch and Jolly Hill, Diamond and Ruby — and The Whim!

Of all these, it is Estate Whim that best tells the visual story of what the "good old days" were like. It is the only restored Greathouse open to the public as a museum. And in addition, the mystery of its name is enhanced by a colorful legend about the man who may have built it.

WHIM GREATHOUSE. Not far from Frederiksted, just off Centerline Road, stands one of St. Croix's really unique structures known both as the Greathouse at John's Rest and as The Whim. It is an exceptional building for St. Croix, designed in neo-classic European style with curved ends and a surrounding "moat" which served as an air shaft for the cellar and as a water runoff area. Apparently there was at one time a stream under the house and this joined the rainwater carried from the "moat" to an underground culvert to a well.

Whim was leased from the Virgin Islands Government and then restored over a period of years by the former St. Croix Museum, under the architectural direction of Mr. William G. Thayer, Jr. of Frederiksted. The Museum is now amalgamated with the Landmarks Society.

Whim is open to the public except Mondays, from 10 to 12 and 2 to 5; Sundays, 2:30 to 5 p.m. It is one of the island's showplaces; a house museum which recreates the opulent life of the sugar planters with their fine furniture, silver and china brought out from Europe in the late 1700's when the island was at the peak of its prosperity.

Much of Whim's original history is lost or obscure, although many later records exist of owners and their sugar production figures. Danish archives have been searched, but little really conclusive evidence exists about its builder, presumably

WHIM GREATHOUSE   By Ralph Fuller

a   Christopher MacEvoy, Jr. The estate dates back to 1751 when it was called merely Plantation #4 Westend. Its name was changed to John's Rest in 1764 when the owner John Delaney was buried on the grounds. Oxholm's map of 1794 shows a house and ox-mill there about the time it was inherited by MacEvoy, Jr.

MacEvoy, Jr. was a flamboyant and ostentatious man, who might well have built the present Greathouse. He had been educated in both England and Denmark and came out to St. Croix when he inherited several estates on the island. Later he moved back to Denmark and bought Bernstorff Castle, plus a palace and sugar-refinery. He was made a Court Chamberlain.

Whether John's Rest was the "whim" of an eccentric, or so-called simply because it had an ox-whim (often called a "whimy" or "the whim") we may never know. In any case, its Greathouse is one of the outstanding and unique buildings on the island.

THE MacEVOY LEGEND.   One of the stories told of MacEvoy in Denmark concerns his desire for grandeur. When he was a Court Chamberlain to King Frederik IV, he once angered the King by having a beautiful carriage with elegant coachmen, pulled by four magnificent white horses. Not only were white horses a privilege afforded only to nobility, the whole equipage was grander than the King's own!

Rebuked, MacEvoy took a long vacation in North America and other distant parts, but returned again to live in Denmark. His journey had not been in vain and he was not idle in exile. When next he drove out in Copenhagen, his coach was finer than ever, and it was drawn not by four white horses, but by eight rare white mules. Each wore fine lace on its head and ears. The lead mules were ridden by two Haiduks in impressive gold-braided uniforms, while a colored major-domo led the parade. A handsome coachman held the reins, while MacEvoy sat in state behind. No picture exists of him to tell if he was as handsome as his equipage.

1

This time the King recognized a kindred regal spirit and forgave his enterprising Chamberlain for his boldness.

Some day we hope to learn for certain whether it was this same audacious MacEvoy who was the actual builder of Whim Greathouse.

ISLAND LIFE. The Danes also governed their islands with a fairly tight rein. Christiansted was at this time the Capitol of the three islands and Government House was the hub of social and commercial life. The Governor-General was appointed for an indefinite period by the home government in Copenhagen. The Governor had a Council to pass ordinances and to advise him, but could veto its decisions. All his final decisions were subject to change in Copenhagen, and many a Governor spent much of his time there justifying his actions or seeking support for his plans.

The structure of the rest of the government was not complicated. There were local courts, local fighting corps under regimental officers sent out from Denmark, Burgher Corps made up of all citizens under sixty years who could bear arms, a Brand Corps of fire-fighters, and civil police. All the military wore impressive uniforms.

Since the English, Scotch and Irish outnumbered the Danes at least five to one in the planter class, English became the everyday spoken language of the schools, commercial and social life: Danish was used in government papers and courts and in the Lutheran Church.

At first the Danes had allowed only the Lutheran and Moravian churches on the island, but relaxed this to include the Anglican, Dutch-Reformed Church and others. A group of Catholics who had settled here from Montserrat once complained bitterly that the Puerto Ricans would not return their escaped slaves on the grounds that there was no priest in St. Croix to minister to them.

The Dutch-Reformed Church played a prominent role in the island religious life, taking an especial interest in the education of the slaves. Many of the Negroes, particularly in St. Thomas, spoke a Creole dialect, and this church translated its hymnal and the New Testament into this "new" language. The Lutheran Church conducted services in Danish and in the dialect.

The commercial life of the island at its peak around 1795 was extensive, but not varied, as it all revolved around sugar, rum and molasses. The dock

KOLONIALADJUTANTERNE c. 1816

area was the focal point of Christiansted and Frederiksted, with the harbor and roadstead teeming with ships of all nations. There were a few mercantile houses which imported the necessities and luxuries, shipping agents, various tradesmen and middlemen. There were the usual lawyers, doctors, ministers and other professional groups. The richest planters built town houses in addition to their country Greathouses, and the building trades flourished, using both freed Negroes and slave labor.

Not a little smuggling went on all during the Danish times, as the English, Scotch and Irish chafed under strict trade restrictions set up in Copenhagen, including heavy export taxes and stiff regulations about inter-island trading.

The English particularly wanted more leeway to trade with North America for much needed lumber, salt fish, barrel staves, hoops and horses. Higher prices were sometimes paid for sugar, rum or molasses in the other islands, and Cruzans were not adverse to extra profits. The Frederiksted Fort had been completed in 1760 to stop smuggling to St. Eustatius, but on this score was more decorative than useful.

Aside from the sugar and rum industry, the most important trade lay in the slave traffic. Originally, the Danish West India and Guinea Company had established its own trading stations on the African coast, but later these were given up when the Danish crown took over administration of the islands. As St. Croix grew and prospered, the number of slaves increased in proportion. Figures are available for some years, and we know that from 1773 to 1791 there were over 21,000 slaves on St. Croix alone. By 1802, there were 27,000.

The Negroes were not treated too badly in the Danish islands since the home government set up very strict laws about their treatment, working hours and provisions. These laws were enforced. Nearly every plantation had its "hospital" for sick workers and lying-in women, and retained a doctor on a yearly fee who came regularly. At Beck's Grove ruin there still stands the estate hospital building — a large one of beautiful proportions still bearing up its massive original stone slab roof.

The Danes provided stringent regulations in the islands to cover most human activities from birth to death. Illustrating this is part of a six-page contract of:

Instructions to Midwives as shown on the opposite page.

Instructions To Midwives

"... above all she shall have God in view and at heart. Lead an honest and pious life, conduct herself friendly and with decency toward everyone, but especially towards those who request her as suppliants for service, be always at hand and always willing, both day and night to serve without delay, as well the poor as the rich, and never to forsake those to whose assistance she has first been called, without a proper cause.

"... she shall likewise lead a sober life and abstain from all strong liquors, as well previous as after the birth of a child, considering that she is liable to be called on at every moment, and that the lives and health of two or more persons depend upon her conduct and faithful treatment.

"She must also be ... faithful, diligent, indefatigable and silent in all her callings which should be kept secret ...

"It will be her duty in every extraordinary and dangerous birth betimes to apply to and consult a skillful and well known physician and to take his advice and opinion on the subject ... she shall not interfere or trouble herself with any other branch of physic, but that she shall be prohibited, on no consideration whatever, to administer remedies, liquids, powders or drugs of any denomination to married or to unmarried women whereby the foetus in the mother's womb, might be injured, killed or expelled, living or dead, nor shall she prepare said remedies or suffer them to be prepared nor give them herself or advise others to do it. Should anyone apply to her for the like advice and remedies, she must carefully and precisely pry into the circumstances and denounce such persons and their intentions to the magistrate.

"... should she ... prove disobedient, heedless, obstinate and unfaithful, or should she not serve with the utmost diligence and exactness to conform to the foregoing orders, she shall be cashiered and moreover shall be liable, according to the nature of the circumstances to be punished with a fine, confiscation of property or the loss of her honor or even her life ..."

St Helena Bermuda

The
St. CROIXIAN
POCKET,
Companion

or

*a brief sketch of the Chief things necessary
to be known by the dwellers in, or
traders to the Island.*

Extracted

from the beſt authorities.

Coppenhagen, 1780.
Printed for the Author.

XIII.
Regulation relating Grave Diggers fees or Charges and funeral Expences; allow'd agreeable to Inſtructions, dated 20 Nov. 1770.

1. No Grave can be dug at the Burying Ground, without the Knowledge and Conſent of the appointed Sexton or Grave Digger.

2. Every Grave beſpoke, shall be finish'd by the ſaid Sexton in the Space of 6 or 8 houres after application, Night excepted. And every Grave for a full grown Corps ſhall be dug 6 feet deep 8 feet long and 4 feet broad. If this is not comply'd, then he shall not only loſe his fees, but pay a fine of 10 Ps. ¾.

3. The Grave shall be dug in any particulair place in the Burying Ground, the parties concern'd shal appoint.

For a Grave made in the Church yard, near the church of England, shall be paid double, owing to the hardneſs of the Ground.

ON THE LIVELIER side of Cruzan life in these prosperous years many events were stirring. The question of halting the slave trade was being discussed in Denmark and in many other European nations. The planters, here and elsewhere, were in the main against this as being against their own best interests. However, in St. Croix any slave who could save the money could buy his freedom and the master was obliged to sell at a court-appraised price. Each Negro family had its own provision ground on the plantation and was allowed to sell the surplus. Consequently, the Danish islands had an extremely high percentage of free Negroes. When the Edict came from the King in 1792 forbidding all Danes from taking part in the slave trade, it came partly because a wealthy planter here, Ernst Schimmelmann of La Grande Princesse, had persuaded the King to take this move. The next Edict came in 1803 after a transition period of some ten years, formally abolishing the slave trade.

None of this made it any easier for those still slave, and the planters lived always in the shadow of fear. There was fear of rebellion or riots, of the cane fields being burned, and the fear of what would happen if the slaves were free.

There was the yearly tension about hurricanes and occasionally the total loss of the sugar crop from one. There were drought, and strange diseases ranging from malaria to cholera to yellow fever, which carried off workers and masters alike.

High insurance rates, debts and mortgages were part of the picture. Planters, wealthy in land and slaves and possessions, were nearly always in some kind of debt. There was debt for expansion of holdings; debt out of necessity to stay in business. There was the eternal borrowing ahead on the next crop. Sometimes there were complicated lawsuits over titles for estates that had many mortgages against them. High taxes were a complaint, then as now.

The trouble was that once set up and going, a sugar plantation was a demanding affair, almost impossible to convert to any other type of plantation. Once in the sugar and rum business, a planter was in it for better or for worse.

Rare was the planter who lolled at his ease before sundown; along with his managers and overseers, he worked and worked hard. The planter's wife supervised her own large work force in the Greathouse and its gardens. She was also expected to minister to the needs of the workers' families.

The Age of Opulence, soon to draw to a close, had its own drawbacks when examined closely.

A RICH MAN'S FORTUNE OR FOLLY

THE actual physical requirements for running a sugar plantation were somewhat staggering, as is best shown by some of the accompanying tables.

In St. Croix, the initial investment was low in comparison to the other islands in which sugar was well established. The Danes wanted quick colonization and quick returns for their West India and Guinea Company. They surveyed the island in 1735, using the present Centerline Road as a base from which the surveys began.

The island was divided into rectangles of 150 Danish acres each, known as Matriculens. The price was $500 for one of these plantations good enough for sugar cane. For cotton land, mostly in the East End, the price was $250 a plantation. There was also a seven year tax exemption for newcomers who took up the "patents" on new plantations.

There were newcomers at these bargain prices, and no wonder that most of them were from nearby British islands where land prices were high. In Jamaica they ran as high as 1,000 pounds sterling for 100 acres.

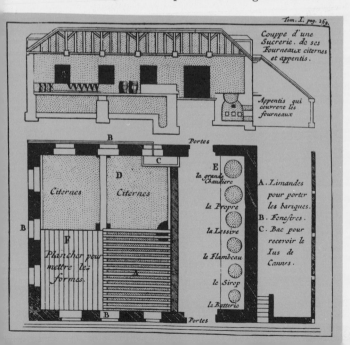

SUGAR FACTORY in 1724

A. Openwork to hold barrels.
B. Windows.
C. Receiver for cane juice.
D. Cisterns for molasses
E. Coppers for boiling sugar
F. Racks for draining molasses.

From Pere Labat

24

Bryan Edwards, who was a British planter in Jamaica and one of the best known early economic historians of the Caribbean, says that it required no less investment than 30,000 pounds sterling minimum just to get a 900 acre plantation set up and that a smaller one would not pay there. (This amount equalled some $120,000 in U.S. dollars at the 1800 exchange rate).

In St. Croix, the planters used about three-fourths of their land for sugar growing and the factory area. The other one-fourth was for houses, pasture and timber. The British divided theirs into thirds — one area for cane, one for pasturage and provision grounds, and one for timber to be used in buildings.

There are no figures on the cost of a Greathouse which depended upon the plain or lavish taste of the owner. In any case, they were built with slave labor, as was the estate village where the workers lived.

In St. Croix, the 300 acres bought for 1,000 Danish rigsdalers in 1734, sold some 15 years later for about 3,400 West Indian rigsdalers v.c. (Special rigsdalers issued in Denmark for island currency. The v.c. meant value current, which fluctuated). It was estimated that it cost nearly 17,000 rigsdalers v.c. to set up a plantation in the earliest years, but later this price must have doubled. A windmill which cost some 2,000 rigsdalers v.c. to build in 1760 had gone up to around 9,000 rigsdalers v.c. some ten years later. By this time the total value of a plantation had risen to between 50,000 to

INITIAL BUILDING COSTS, not including Greathouse or Negro Quarters

1.	Mill	1,400
2.	Boiling House	1,000
3.	Curing House	900
4.	Distilling House	1,600
5.	Overseer's House	600
6.	2 storehouses	600
7.	Hospital	300
8.	Mule stable	150
9.	Workshop for carpenters, Wheelwrights & blacksmiths	150
10.	Sheds	50
11.	Tools, Furniture, Utensils	350
	Totals: Jamaica currency	7,100
	in Pounds Sterling	5,000
	in U.S. (1800 rate)	$20,000

ANNUAL COSTS on Coppers, Stills, Waintyres, Grating Bars, Freight & Commissions.
8,501 pounds sterling

ANNUAL CONTINGENT CHARGES:

Overseers or manager's salary	200
Distiller's salary	70
2 other white servants	120
Maintenance 5 white servants	200
Carpenter's wages	100
Medical care of negroes	100
Millwright, coppersmith, smith & plumber	250
Colonial taxes	200
Mules & Steers annually	300
Wharfage & storage	100
Staves & heading for hogsheads & puncheons	150
Miscellaneous	50
Totals: Jamaica currency	1,840
in Pounds Sterling	1,300
in U.S. (1800 rate)	$5,200

25

ANNUAL SUPPLIES

Negro Clothing:
1,500 yds. Oznaburgh cloth
  650 yds. blue bays or pennistones
  350 yds. striped linseys
  250 yds. coarse check for shirts
    3 dz. coarse blankets
   18 dz. coarse hats

TOOLS: For carpenters, coopers, to amt. of 25 pounds sterling, including 2 or 3 dz. of falling axes.

MISCELLANEOUS:
160,000 nails
  2,500 puncheon rivets
     50 bundles iron hoops
    180 ditto wood hoops
     80 gal. train oil
      6 cattle chains
      6 dozen of hoes
      6 dozen of bills (cane knives)
      4 dozen of ox bows
      2 sets puncheon hoops
      2 sets hogshead ditto
      2 sheets of lead
      6 large copper ladles
      6 ditto skimmers
     20 dz. small clasp knives
      2 barrels of tar
      2 boxes short tobacco
      8 dz. small iron pots
      4 grindstones
      2 puncheons Bristol lime

PROVISIONS:
     80 barrels herring or salt
        cod equal thereto
      6 barrels salted beef
      2 barrels salted pork
      4 firkins salted butter
      2 boxes of soap
      2 boxes of candles
      2 hogshead of salt
      6 barrels of flour
      6 kegs of pease
      3 jugs of groats

70,000 rigsdalers v.c. according to what the planter could invest. Many things contributed to the rise, including the higher land prices and the need for more slaves to work an established plantation. Lacking other specific figures for St. Croix, it is interesting to consider what Bryan Edwards said was needed to set up a 900 acre sugar plantation on a British island. As a preliminary, he warned, "the man that engages in the business of sugar planting must engage deeply. There is no medium and very seldom the possibility of retreat."

"The price for clearing, cultivating and fencing will run up to 10,000 pounds sterling.

"The upkeep of a plantation of the magnitude described cannot prudently be considered without the aid of 250 negroes annually, plus a stock of 60 mules and 80 steers:

250 negroes @ 70 pounds each	17,500
60 mules @ 28 pounds each	1,680
80 mules @ 15 pounds each	1,200
	20,380 pounds Jamaica currency

(this equalled 14,557 pounds sterling, or approximately $58,000 U.S. at the 1800 rate).

WHEN the hard work was done, the plantation a going business, and the planter ready to loll at his ease at sundown with a planter's punch resting on the arm of one of those old planters' chairs, this is what he could expect, according to historian Edwards:

"The produce of such a plantation is approximately 200 hogsheads of sugar of 16cwt, at 3,000 pounds sterling; 130 puncheons of rum at 1,300 pounds sterling (average price on the London market for 10 years) which makes a gross return of pounds sterling 4,300.

"But the reader is not to imagine that all this, even the sugar alone, is clear profit. The annual disbursements are first to be deducted and very heavy they are, with the charges within the island and the annual supplies amounting to some 2,150 pounds sterling, leaving no more clear profit to the planter than seven per cent. And this is without charging, however, a shilling for making good the decrease of the negroes, or for the wear and tear of the buildings, or making allowance for dead capital.

"In short, with these and other drawbacks, to say nothing of the devastations which are sometimes occasioned by fires and hurricanes, it is not wonderful that the profits should frequently dwindle to nothing, or rather that a sugar estate, with all its boasted advantages, should sometimes *prove a millstone* about the neck of its unfortunate proprietor, which is dragging him to destruction."

Just how hard the planter worked for his seven percent gross return will be seen in the process he had to go through to make the sugar and the rum.

CANE PLANTING

ST. CROIX'S SUGAR MILLS

THE island's picturesque old windmills and animal mills which dot its landscape were mostly built early in the period of 1750 to 1800. A few estates had two windmills, and in addition many had auxiliary ox or mule mills. For when the cane was ready it must be cut, and when it was cut it must be ground quickly to avoid fermentation. During "crop" speed was essential; the mills ground incessantly, day and night, with the men working in shifts.

THE ANIMAL MILL. This consisted of the central grinding machinery under a shed surrounded by an earthenwork or stonework elevated rim, with the appearance of a circular crater. Along the top of the rim the oxen, mules or horses walked on a path. A long pole ran from the animals' harness to the center shaft of the machinery, thus turning it and providing the power for the grinding.

The earliest animal mills did well if they ground enough canes in one hour to yield from 300 to 350 gallons of juice. Later models using up to ten mules, produced some 500 gallons an hour. Allowing four hours out of the twenty-four for

Courtesy "Vore Gamle Tropekolonier"

EARLY ANIMAL MILL

A. Cattle being driven to turn mill machinery. B. The big roller of the machinery. C. Small rollers which grind cane. D. Pipe through which juice drains. E. Tub which receives the juice. F. Two vessels of water which drips on rollers to prevent friction. G. Center gear of big roller which makes the machine turn. H. Wooden framework to support machinery. I. Board on which sugar cane is placed. J. Cauldrons or Coppers in which juice is boiled.

loss of time, the return per day could be
10,000 gallons of juice, being equal to 36
hogsheads of sugar at 16-cwt. for every week
during the crop season.

THE WINDMILL—HOW IT WORKED.

A windmill is essentially a simple contriv-
ance, yet great force is required to run it
to overcome the resistance of the cane being
ground. In the early days in St. Croix, the
machinery inside the mill consisted princi-
pally of three upright iron-plated rollers or
cylinders. The middle one, to which the
moving-power was attached from above,
turned the other two by means of cogs.

Between these rollers the canes were com-
pressed. They passed through the first and
second rollers; were turned around the center one by a circular framework or screen
sometimes called the "dumb returner," and
were forced back through the second and
third rollers.

This operation squeezed the cane nearly
dry. The juice ran downhill in a leaded
trough to the factory below. The leftover
fibre refuse, called *bagasse* was later used
as fuel under the coppers in which the juice
was boiled.

The St. Croix mills were a Dutch type,
in which only the dome was turned, carrying the axle and sails with it into the required position. The masonry top of the
mill had a wooden (later cast iron) rim on
which ran small rollers on which the dome
rested. The turning of the dome, so that the

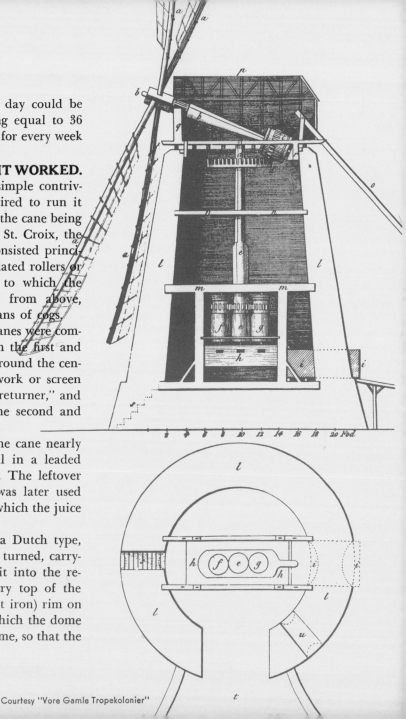

STEAM MILL at ANNA'S HOPE

four canvas sails on their wooden arms would face directly into the wind, was accomplished by means of a long pole at an angle running down nearly to the ground from the dome. A whole crew of men sometimes had to rush to shift the pole when the wind blew stronger or changed direction.

The problems of controlling the sails to give an even grinding operation were not easily solved. There was at first no means of reefing, and sometimes a gusty wind revolved it all so fast that the sails were torn off. Later, a way was devised for men to climb up to reef the sails individually.

The first successful automatic reefing apparatus was invented in 1780, giving controlled motion to the grinding for the first time. In 1807, a further improved method of reefing the big sails was introduced. This was a simple arrangement of movable wooden shutters or louvers in part of the sails instead of canvas.

Today on St. Croix these stone windmills are highly prized for their haunting quality of beauty and as reminders of the special historic heritage of the island. Much of the old machinery was sold for scrap or lies rusting in the underbrush. The mill at Whim Greathouse is being restored to working order by the Landmarks Society so that visitors and islanders can visualize its use.

THE STEAM MILLS. The first steam mill for grinding cane was put in use at Estate Hogansborg for the crop of 1816, but it was so balky and broke down so often that other plantation owners remained unconvinced that steam was worth the expense. It was not until the 1830's that other steam mills made their appearance at Whim and another estate. Wind power and slaves were still cheaper than steam.

However, just four years after the slaves were freed in 1848, there were some fifty steam engines here.

In the yard of La Grange stands a piece of narrow-gauge railway track with a small type of flatcar on it. This is one of the last remnants of a little rail line which once ran along the northwest shore carrying cane to La Grange factory. Another, south shore, railway led to the factory at Bethlehem which served the estates in the center of the island. Reportedly, the entire track, tiny steam engine and strings of flatcars were sold years ago to Mexico.

In 1876, the Danish government underwrote the building of five large cane crushing stations at Estates Fair Plain, Glynn, Barren Spot, La Grande Princess and at Peter's Rest, which was the largest station. From these estates, cane juice was pumped through miles of pipe lines to huge tanks at Orange Grove where Cruzana now is, and on down to a Central Factory on the shore near Christiansted.

Today all the island's cane is ground at the huge complex known as Bethlehem Factory near the center of the island. Tomorrow — who knows — the grinding of cane commercially on the island may come to a final stop after three hundred and some years.

SUGAR HAULING ON CENTERLINE ROAD

Early day scene near Estate Bethlehem of hogsheads of sugar on their way to the Christiansted wharf; drawn by six oxen.

Courtesy
"Vore Gamle Tropekolonier"

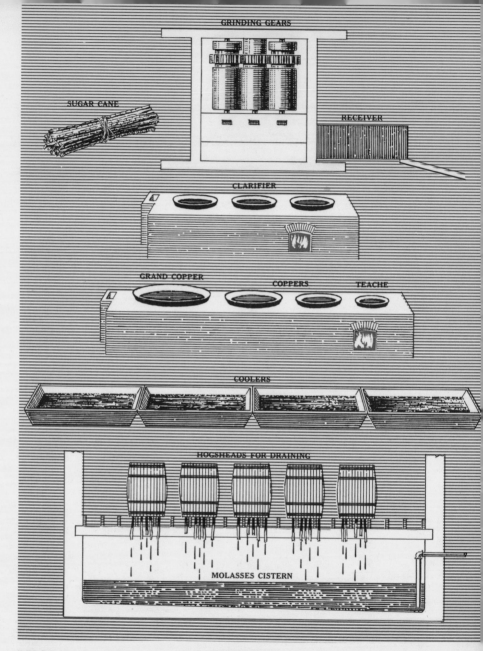

GRINDING GEARS

SUGAR CANE

RECEIVER

CLARIFIER

GRAND COPPER   COPPERS   TEACHE

COOLERS

HOGSHEADS FOR DRAINING

MOLASSES CISTERN

DIAGRAM OF SUGAR MAKING PROCESS

By Ralph Fuller

HOW SUGAR WAS MADE

THE cut cane was carted in from the fields to the mill; cut short and bundled for the grinders.

The cane was put through the mill's grinding machinery; the juices ran into the big vessel called the *Receiver*.

The juice ran out of the Receiver into a leaded trough, downhill to the Factory into a large vessel called:

The *Clarifier,* of which there were as many as three holding 300 to 400 gallons each. Fire was lighted under the Clarifier, a temper added, such as Bristol lime powder (or a vegetable alkali or ashes of certain woods).

Scum rose to the top as the juice was brought almost to a boil. Damper applied and fire extinguished. The juice remained there an hour while impurities collected on top. Each Clarifier had a siphon or cock for drawing off juice, which then went by gutter to:

The *Grand Copper* or evaporating boiler where juice was boiled and the rising scum taken off with large skimmers. When thickened, the juice was ladled into the smaller or *Second Copper*. Boiling and skimming continued; perhaps lime-water added to temper the juice and to dilute thickness.

The process was repeated in the *Third Copper;* then it was ladled into the

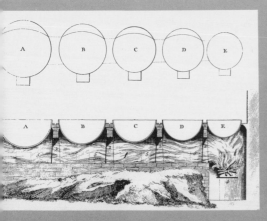

COPPERS and FURNACE   From Diderot   SUGAR BOILING IN COPPERS   From Diderot

Fourth Copper, called the *Teache,* where the final evaporation was done. The juice was now very thick, and tested in cold water for coagulation. Small plantations sometimes used only two coppers for the process. When ready, the juice was ladled, called taking a *strike,* into:

The *Cooler,* of which there were usually six. These were shallow, wooden vessels, about 7' long and 5' to 6' wide. Each held one hogshead (1,600 lbs.) of sugar. In the cooler, the sugar *grained;* i.e., as it cooled, it formed a coarse mass of crystals, separating from the molasses residue. It was then:

Carried to the *Curing house* where the molasses was to be drained out. The Curing house consisted of a molasses cistern with sloping sides of terras or boards. Over the cistern an open framework of joists held rows of hogsheads, each with 8 to 10 holes in the bottom, each hole plugged with a plantain stalk through which molasses drained.

The mass from the cooler was put into hogsheads, which was termed *potting,* and allowed to drain through the pulpy stalks for about three weeks. By then the grains were dry and ready for shipment. This made a brown sugar, called *Muscovado.*

A system of *claying* or further refining sugar was sometimes used. The sugar and molasses mass from the cooler was poured into conical pots or pans, suspended points downward with a hole in the point. This hole was kept plugged for 12 hours during the cooling, then opened and the molasses drained out for another 12 to 24 hours.

Then a mixture of *clay* was spread on top the sugar; some water added to seep down through the clay to carry off more molasses. This left a pure, white sugar.

WIND and STEAM

MOLASSES TO RUM TO PLANTER'S PUNCH

R U M has gone by many names: Rhum, Rumm, Rumbooze, Rhumb and Rum-bullion — and even the Indians had a word for it — Ahcoobee.

As almost every West Indian knows, no two rums taste quite the same, varying greatly from island to island. In the early days on St. Croix, the quality of rum even varied from estate to estate. Each planter had his favorite methods and his secrets of flavor for creating what he felt was the superior product.

The making of sugar and the making of rum were inseparable. Each planta-tion had its own still house, usually next to the sugar factory, where the molasses was used for rum-making. On St. Croix, the rum-making was on a fairly simple scale, but on the huge plantations of some of the British islands rum was also made on a grand scale with elaborate equipment.

HOW POT STILL RUM WAS MADE. The *still house* in which the rum was made contained a number of large wood-en vats called *butts,* generally 10 or 12 of them averaging from 750 to 1,000 gallons capacity. Copper *pot-stills* with a capacity approximately the same as a butt were located outside of the still house to accommodate the wood fires which heated the pots. An open shed covered the distilling equipment to keep rain off. In the bottom of each butt there

FRENCH BRANDY POT STILL   From Diderot

was a 2 inch hole stoppered with a long wooden plug. This was removed when fermentation was complete (in from 4 to 6 days) and the fermented *mash* ran down in wooden troughs to the pot-still.

Three types of mash were used for fermentation: the chief one being a mixture of about one part molasses to five parts water, to which was sometimes added *cush-cush,* the fine *Bagasse* particles left in the strainer when the cane juice ran

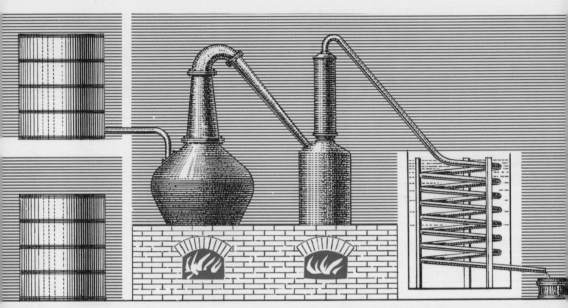

DIAGRAM OF POT STILL RUM PROCESS

down from the mill. This was used as a *yeast* or *mother*. To this was usually added some form of acid, and some lime or vegetable ash. When all this was fermented, it was ready for use.

The second type of fermentation could be used only during crop time, usually before any molasses was available from the new crop. It was pure cane juice direct from the mill, requiring no special additives to start fermentation as the juice contained *wild yeast*, the whitish powder found around the knot or joint of the cane stalk.

The third fermented mixture came from using all the skimmings from the sugar process, added to the molasses. This also could be done only during crop time.

Next to the pot-still and elevated to about the same level, connected by a gooseneck pipe, sat the *doubler* or retort; usually made of wood. It had another connecting pipe which ran to the final piece of equipment, the pewter *worms* or coils of pipe which were suspended in a large cistern of cold water.

When all was ready, the pot-still was filled with fermented mash; the doubler filled to about ¼ its capacity with *low wine,* a weak low-proof rum which comes at the beginning and end of each distillation. The doubler usually had about 100 to 150 gallons of low wine in it.

The two vessels were closed and fire started under the pot-still. As the mash cooked, the resulting vapors went over into the doubler by the gooseneck which went down to within two or three inches of the bottom. These hot vapors in turn started the low-wine boiling and these combined vapors gained much in alcohol or proof strength, passing on into the pewter worms. The hot vapors running down through the cold pewter worms condensed into the liquid known as rum, and ran into a receiving vessel — always a wooden tub, usually made by cutting down a puncheon.

Approximately the first five gallons of the condensed liquid were drawn off as low-wine to put back into the doubler as they retained some of the low quality condensate from the tail end of the previous distillation.

Once this was done, the rum began to run at about 140° proof and ran until the proof dropped to about 108°. From this one run there would come about 100 wine gallons of rum with an average proof of about 120°.

When the proof dropped below 108°, the rum was "cut" which meant that the distillate coming out was too inferior for rum and was accumulated as low-wine. This was run out until there were about 100 to 150 wine gallons of low-wine which were put back into the low-wine butt to be used to charge the doubler again for the next distillation.

The operation was then stopped. The exhausted low-wine in the doubler was run back into the pot-still and together with all the used fermented mash in the pot, known as the *lees,* was run out into the *lees pond* outside the still house and discarded. The process was then ready to start all over again.

A LITTLE RUM-INATION.   Every planter had his own opinion about making rum and the variations were endless. While the best rum came from cane juice alone, it was also the most expensive process, and today there are only two or three brands in all the West Indies made this way.

The early planters were known to use such flavor pickups as Seville oranges, lemons, tamarinds or any acid fruit. The St. Kitts distillers added sea water and swore by it. Others used nitre, tartar, common salt, vegetable or mineral acids.

The vegetable ashes supposedly kept back the heavy and fetid oil known by the British makers as the *faints*, but this also tended to keep back the fine, essential oils which flavored the rum. Another trick was to put back a few gallons of the high-proof distillate into the fermentation vats, which was supposed to add greatly to the quantity of the next rum.

The quality of the cane and its sweet content, known as *Brix*, also had a bearing on rum-making. The market demand, too, had a direct bearing. If the price of sugar were high and that of rum low, the distiller would return more of the skimmings and other sugar-containing matter to the sugar clarifiers instead of sending them to the still house. This way they gained in sugar value what they lost in rum. This practice could be reversed to make more or better rum and less sugar.

In the early days, the distiller used to test the rum for proof by taking it in his hand and smelling it, or by shaking it to judge the bead on a high proof. The British islanders used an "oil proof" test in which olive oil sank in high proof rum.

The rum was stored and shipped in large casks called puncheons, of variable size from island to island, but usually holding from 110 to 150 wine gallons. On St. Croix they used a 140 gallon puncheon.

The British estimated the production of whole rum to finished sugar as approximately three to four. Always the individualists, the British also called their molasses, *treacle;* their lees, *dunder;* and their skimmings, *scummings.* They did call the product rum! They also did what distillers on the other islands thought was inexcusable — they put a small percentage of the lees or dregs of the process back into their fermenation vats. It may have been this practice that earned some rum the nickname of "kill devil."

The rums made on the island of St. Croix today are vastly different and better than the variable and heavy type of yesteryear. They are now made on a large scale in *continuous column stills* under highly controlled methods and exact processes, including the careful removal of the *fusel oils* and *heads,* resulting in a uniform, dry, light quality rum of excellent flavor and bouquet.

CONCLUSION: Truly, the Rums of St. Croix are so good that there must be some special secrets in their manufacture.

YE OLDE RUM DRINKS

CALIBOGUS OR BOGUS

A combination of cold rum and beer.

STONEWALL

A mixture of cider and rum.

GROG

A mixture of rum and water. Named for Admiral Vernon of the British Navy who walked around in a grogam or gros-grain cloak. The Admiral laced the "neat" rum ration with water, and his sailors called their rations by his nickname "Old Grog." George Washington's half-brother, Lawrence, served with Vernon and later named the family estate Mt. Vernon.

TODDY

Also called Bombo. A favorite drink of rum, hot water and sugar served with a long toddy stick with a knob on the end to crush the loaf sugar. The word Toddy is a corruption of the East Indian *tandi,* the word for the sweet juice of palm spathes.

BUB

Take a quantity of rum, sweeten it well with sugar, milk a cow into it; it will curdle; skim it off; then milk into it again, and it makes a delicious beverage.

GREEN SWIZZLE

A famous West Indian drink of rum and green bitters, plus a few drops of wormwood, the base of absinthe. Its effect is potent and two is the limit.

BLACKSTRAP

A combination of rum and molasses with vinegar and other ingredients.

SWITCHEL

A favorite sailor's drink of molasses, water, vinegar and rum.

PUNCH

A combination of tea, sugar, lemons, water and rum. The name comes from the Hindustani *panch* meaning five, for their ingredients of tea, Arrack or distilled date or palm juice, sugar, lemons and water. The West Indians substituted rum for the Arrack.

MISS BLYDEN

A combination of sugar, rum and the juice of prickly pear, bottled and buried in the ground until seasoned.

RUM AND REVOLUTION

T H E relationship between West Indian rum and the American Revolution is one often ignored by the history books, perhaps because its story is not the most savory. It is a complicated tale of smuggling, slave trading and evasion of the British Acts of Trade — all of which were respectable New England occupations at the time.

The British Molasses Act of 1733, the New Molasses Act of 1765 and the 1765 Stamp Act set up an economic chain of events leading directly to the Revolution. In effect the New Molasses Act prevented the North Americans from trading with the French, Dutch and Danish islands for molasses by imposing a stiff duty, and as a consequence would have forced the New Englanders to abandon their rum stills and buy rum from the British West Indies. The effect on the rum distillers (63 in Massachusetts alone) was incalculable, as it was tied directly to the whole economic structure of the area, based on the rum and slave trade.

The British themselves had been in the slave trade since 1562 to supply their own Caribbean colonies and those of Spain. In the 106 years from 1680 to 1786 there were some 2,130,000 slaves imported into their southern American and West Indian colonies. There were few slaves in New England, but this area flourished on the trade, sometimes flouting the laws of Old England to do so.

It all worked on what might be called the Vicious Triangle. New England ships carried their rum and a few other supplies to the West Coast of Africa, where they traded for Negroes and gold dust. From there they made the infamous "middle passage" with their victims crowded in miserable, unhealthy conditions to Barbados and the other British islands where the surviving slaves were sold for cash or bills of credit. The ships then usually picked up cheap contraband molasses at the French and Dutch islands and carried it back to New England to be distilled into rum.

The New England rum was consumed at home in quantities unbelievable to those brought up on a Puritan version of history. Still, there was adequate surplus to ship to Africa.

The smuggling and violations of British regulations arose mainly out of the molasses trade. Sugar was the main West Indian product, but its value and market fluctuated widely, and the planters depended on molasses or rum for the difference between profit and loss.

The French protected their European brandy interests by selling molasses very cheaply in their islands, as did the Dutch who acted as middlemen and were the leading Caribbean merchants. The British regulations were so complicated that they merely led to smuggling between islands. It was the perpetual imbalance of trade with England which made the colonists both in New England and in the islands feel not only justified, but obligated, to evade the rules.

The planters in St. Croix were compelled by a 1740 law to sell their molasses, sugar and rum to the Danish West India Company at less than one-half the price offered in the Dutch free port of St. Eustatius. This same year, the construction of Frederiksted Fort was begun, specifically to stop the smuggling to the Dutch. Then later, during the actual Revolutionary period, this tiny Dutch island became temporarily the richest port in the Caribbean, and the hub of the supply line for the battling northern colonists until 1780. In 1779 alone over 3,500 ships put in at St. Eustatius.

The New England Britishers also supplied the various islands with barrel staves, horses, salted and dried fish from Newfoundland, and other plantation necessities. They were paid in molasses or rum by the French, Dutch and Danish, and in sterling by the British islanders. Other shiploads of dried fish

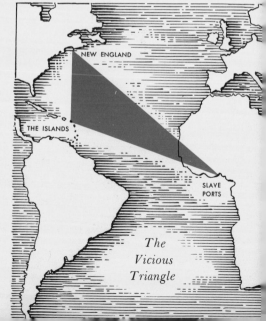

NEW ENGLAND

THE ISLANDS

SLAVE PORTS

The Vicious Triangle

41

By Ralph Fuller

went to Spain and Portugal for gold and silver payment which helped out on the balance of trade. Between times, they supplied the southern colonies of Virginia and the Carolinas with New England products, rum and slaves.

In 1773 Europe was in another of its states of tension over quarrels between various combinations of nations. The price of sugar fell, the coffee market crashed in Germany and a general slump culminated in England's trying to enforce the Tea Tax in the colonies. That was the year of the Boston Tea Party, which in any preceding year might just as well have been a molasses or rum party. It led to the outbreak of actual fighting in 1775.

England promptly switched from French brandy to West Indian rum for its navy, and the French began their unofficial aid to the northern colonies. In the West Indies the smuggling went right on.

The British West Indies were in poor condition to withstand war, long hoped for by Spain and France. Both were ready to fight England or help England's colonies to fight her. According to British historians, Parry and Sherlock, "war against France had long been regarded (by the colonists) as a panacea for the economic ills of the British West Indies, but war against North America was a major disaster, which the West Indian interests in London did their utmost to prevent . . . there were many close connections between the two groups of colonists . . . sympathies were divided. . . ."

"The American rebels tried hard to persuade the West Indies to join in the Revolution, and at first there was some force in the arguments they used:

"The British West Indies had constitutions similar to those in the rebellious thirteen colonies; they had some representative but not responsible government; they had largely the same grievances of taxation without representation, interference with their legislative freedom, and adverse trade balances, the inconveniences and restrictions of the Acts of Trade.

"Like the North Americans, many West Indians rioted against the Stamp Act. Like North America, the West Indies were taxed to pay part of the imperial defense, but there lay the difference. The North American colonies believed that

SLAVE SHIPS

42

they did not need the defense for which they were asked to pay. The West Indies *did* need it, and *knew* they needed it."

The British West Indies finally refused to join in our Revolution. The people "smuggled and grumbled and hoped the war would be short." France went in officially against England in 1778; took Dominica, and next year took Grenada and St. Vincent. Spain went in in 1779, mainly to seize and plunder the British islands.

There is an undocumented story that the first salute to the new United States flag was given at Frederiksted Fort on St. Croix.

At The Hague in 1780, John Adams persuaded the Dutch to recognize our independence. The British promptly declared war on the Dutch, and Admiral Rodney took St. Eustatius. He called this free port a nest of villains which needed scourging. Finding at least 125 ships of all nations there, he seized them all and sold both ships and cargoes for over $25,000,000 in one of the world's biggest auctions. This caused a wave of protests from other governments and an impressive legal tangle over ownerships. However, Rodney had cut the main supply line to the north and had relegated tiny St. Eustatius back to a sleepy normal.

The French fleet, released after the Yorktown surrender, went into action in the Caribbean under de Grasse and took many islands. Spain moved in on Florida and the Bahamas. The Caribbean became the final battleground after the American Revolution was over.

AFTER THE REVOLUTION.

The aftermath was again a story of rum and slave trading, depressions and trouble. This was reflected in St. Croix where over half the island was in cane, but 40% of the holdings were in debt, even at this time of good production.

Great Britain outlawed the slave trade, but kept up its West African trading by buying through Spain and Brazil, thus nullifying its own law.

43

FREDERIKSTED FORT   By Amy Jones

The New United States imported six million gallons of West Indian rum by 1818, and also over seven million gallons of molasses used to make rum. Nothing seemed to deter the New England shipowners. As soon as the Revolution was over they had gone right back to a steady course on the old Vicious Triangle. It was not until the Civil War in the United States that slave trading and slavery itself were effectively stopped there, although gradually the New Englanders withdrew from the trade. Rum's tie-in with slave trading ceased to be one of the controlling economic factors in North American life only when the Triangle trade faded away.

Even George Washington succumbed to the custom of mixing rum with politics. In 1758 he ran for the Virginia House of Burgesses from Frederick County during the French and Indian Wars when he was away on the frontier. Leaving his campaign to friends, he arranged for the free dispensing of liquor. The final election returns showed that he got the highest number cast for any candidate. He also had quite a high bar bill!

976 His Excellency Geo. Washington, Esq.
            To Gab. Maupin Dr.
40 gallons of Rum Punch @ 3/6 per gal.
15 " of Wine @ 10/ per galn.
Dinner for Your Friends
13½ gallons of Wine @ 10/
13 gallons of Beer @ 1/3
8 Qts. Cyder Royal @ 1/6
30 galns. of strong Beer @ 8 d.
1 hogshead & 1 barrell of Punch of
    26 galn. best Barbados Rum @ 6/
12 lbs. S. Refined Sugar @ 1/6
10 Bowls of Punch @ 2/6
9 half pints of Rum @ 7½ d. ea.
1 pint of Wine

A. HAMILTON
ON ST. CROIX

S O M E two hundred years ago there was born on Nevis in the British islands a somewhat small, frail and intense boy with blue eyes and red hair. He was the son of an impecunious third son of a Scottish Laird, and of Rachel Lavien. The date of his birth is now set at 1755 by newly discovered Danish documents. This makes Alexander Hamilton two years older than was thought.

His mother, Rachel, had been married some years before in St. Croix at Estate Grange to a much older and cruel husband, John Michael Lavien, who owned a small sugar plantation here. After five years of marriage and the bearing of one son to Lavien, Rachel left him when she was 21. With her mother she moved back to her old home on Nevis where she met James Hamilton. The two fell in love and moved to St. Kitts to live together. Lavien refused Rachel a divorce.

Times were bad financially in parts of the Caribbean and James Hamilton found it hard to make a living for his family. He was sent to St. Croix on a legal mission and Rachel came with him, bringing their two sons. After some months, Hamilton returned to the British islands and Rachel stayed on here with relatives, opening a small shop where the boy Alexander helped out.

When Alexander was eleven he was recognized as being unusually precocious despite lack of much schooling, and he was given work by a hardware merchant, Nicholas Cruger, in his store.

Meanwhile, Lavien had divorced Rachel but Danish law forbade her to remarry. She died on St. Croix when Alexander was thirteen and her gravestone can be visited today at Estate Grange. All her property was claimed by her divorced husband.

Alexander worked hard and read incessantly. He taught himself French, which came in handy later when as aide-de-camp to George Washington he became friends with Generals Lafayette and Rochambeau.

St. Croix was devastated by a major hurricane which destroyed or damaged some 500 buildings in 1772 and Alexander wrote a long and vivid letter to his father on St. Vincent island describing the horror. The letter was published in the Royal Danish-American Gazette, and so impressed friends and others that they scraped together enough money to send him on his way to school in the British Colonies in North America.

Young Hamilton left in mid-summer for Boston on the ship "Thunderbolt" en-route for New York. On the way the ship caught fire and he helped to battle it for twenty-four hours until it was under control.

On his arrival, Alexander went to a boarding school for one year and then entered the already famous King's College (now Columbia University) which at the time had a faculty of only three persons.

In a few short years the ambitious boy became a leader in the Revolution and played a major part in the formation of the original thirteen United States of which he became the first Secretary of the Treasury.

Following are excerpts from the long description of the hurricane which gave Alexander Hamilton his start toward fame.

HURRICANE

Courtesy "Vore Gamle Tropekolonier"

ROYAL DANISH
AMERICAN GAZETTE.

| Vol. I. | WEDNESDAY, January 23, 1771 | No. 68 |

Honored Sir. I take up my pen just to give you an imperfect account of the most dreadful hurricane that memory or any records whatever can trace, which happened here on the 31st ultimo at night.

It began about dusk, at North, and raged very violently till ten o'clock. Then ensued a sudden and unexpected interval, which lasted about an hour. Meanwhile, the wind was shifting round to the South West point, from whence it returned with redoubled fury and continued so till near three o'clock in the morning. Good God! what horror and destruction — it's impossible for me to describe — or you to form any idea of it. It seemed as if a total dissolution of nature was taking place. The roaring of the sea and wind—fiery meteors flying about in the air — the prodigious glare of almost perpetual lightning — the crash of the falling houses — and the ear-piercing shrieks of the distressed, were sufficient to strike astonishment into Angels. A great part of the buildings throughout the Island are leveled to the ground — almost all the rest was very shattered — several persons killed and numbers utterly ruined — whole families running about the streets unknowing where to find a place of shelter — the sick exposed to the keenness of water and air — without a bed to lie upon — or a dry covering to their bodies — our harbour is entirely bare. In a word, misery in all its most hideous shapes spread over the whole face of the country — a strong smell of gunpowder added somewhat to the terrors of the night; and it was observed that the rain was surprisingly salt. Indeed, the water is so brackish and full of sulphur that there is hardly any drinking it.

My reflections and feelings on this frightful and melancholy occasion are set forth in following self-discourse.

Where now OH! Vile worm, is all thy boasted fortitude and sufficiency? — why dost thou tremble and stand aghast? how humble — how helpless — how contemptible you now appear. And for why? the jarring of the elements — the discord of clouds? Oh, impotent presumptuous fool! how darest thou offend that omnipotence, whose nod alone were sufficient to quell the destruction that hovers over thee, or crush thee into atoms? See thy wretched helpless state and learn to know thyself ...

Hark! ruin and confusion on every side. — 'Tis thy turn next: but one short moment — even now — Oh Lord help — Jesus be merciful!

Thus did I reflect, and thus at every gust of the wind did I conclude. — till it pleased the Almighty to allay it.

I am afraid, sir, you will think this description more the effort of imagination than a true picture of realities. But I can affirm with the greatest truth, that there is not a single circumstance touched upon which I have not absolutely been an eyewitness to.

Letter Written By Alexander Hamilton To His Father After The St. Croix Hurricane of 1772

The Warf of St. Croix.

CENTURY OF CHANGE

ST. CROIX in the 19th Century experienced a great period of social change; much for the better on the human level, worse on the economic. It was a time of alternating violence and quiet decline.

At the turn of the century the island was still in a period of upswing. This was marked by the abolition of the slave trade effective in 1803, thus beginning the long, slow progression toward freedom for all. There was soon an Edict of full equality between the free-colored and the white people; later another Edict set up free compulsory education for all children.

Denmark, which had so long remained neutral in most of the European conflicts, found herself and her colonies deeply involved during the Napoleonic Wars.

The English took St. Croix in April of 1801 and held it for about a year. Then there were five years under the Danes again until the British came back in 1807 and stayed for eight years. Little is known of this period of British occupation here. It has been surmised that since most of the planters were English, it may actually have been to their advantage to be out from under what they called restrictive trade laws imposed by Denmark.

St. Croix was returned to Denmark by treaty. The next decades would have been difficult ones under any ownership. A period of increasing depression set in throughout the Caribbean from 1820 on, influenced by European wars and failing economies with a general slump in sugar, rum, tobacco, coffee and other markets. This was reflected in mounting debts in all the islands.

Denmark tried to help St. Croix by making it open to free trade in 1833, a move the planters had long hoped for. Thus began here the free port system which still exists.

Then there came on the scene in St. Croix an energetic, ambitious and capable man who was to influence this island as few others had.

GOVERNOR-GENERAL PETER VON SCHOLTEN.

This dynamic man was not new to the Danish islands. He had come out first at age twenty as a young Danish ensign. Later he returned as a Captain and as the "Royal Weigher." In less than ten years he moved up the ladder of government posts to be Governor of St. Thomas, and was made a Danish Court Chamberlain. Then for eight years he was the acting Governor-General of the three islands.

The outstanding quality in von Scholten was his ability to keep harmony among the diverse groups on the islands. He was considered the best Governor St. Thomas had ever had. While there he learned the Creole language of the Negroes, and became a great helper of the slave population.

It was about the time of his acting Governorship that he fell in love with and took as mistress the lovely free-colored woman, Anna Elisabeth Heegaard. She served as his hostess both for private and public functions and shared his life for twenty years.

Peter and Anna built a gracious mansion at Bulow's

By C. E. Taylor

49

Minde high on the hills overlooking Christiansted. There is some evidence that she paid most of the cost of the house, and the deed was in both their names.

The harmony of life at Bulow's Minde is described in a letter written by a guest of von Scholten's in 1841:

> The main building, which elsewhere would be called a Castle, its light construction not withstanding, has two floors with finely furnished social, dining and dancing rooms and also living quarters for Scholten alone. Adjoining and united to it by a gallery lay Miss Heegaard's, his housekeeper's house, to which the kitchen and other housekeeping quarters belong, then some scattered negro houses; and farthest to the north lay a long, narrow one-story house with windows on both sides and a veranda or covered gallery on which doors from all the rooms opened. This house was divided into several bedrooms and a pair of rooms for visitors — or rather guestrooms.

> The garden lay on the slopes east of and around Scholten's own residence and the guest house, with a profusion of oleanders, hibiscus and other flowers; humming birds swarmed around them like bees at home, and a delightful smell of vanilla reached one when the wind stirred the oleander leaves. The early morning was beautiful and refreshing beyond all description up here in this open and healthfully located place. . . .

> I worked, wrote or read, until I was called to lunch at Scholten's at 9 a.m. where I almost always met one or more adjutants, government officials, or planters who had come to him on business. Lunch, which consisted of tea, several cold and hot dishes, fruit, and wine, was served in Miss Heegaard's rooms, and she and an aging Miss Gordon presided at table.

> Between 1 and 3 p.m. we all went riding, read newspapers, took a short nap on the bed, dressed and gathered at 4 or 5 in Scholten's rooms for dinner. There were always some guests so that we were most often six or more persons. The two women were never missing, and, after the meal, the company, at least those who knew them, paid a short visit to Miss Heegaard's house. We smoked cigars, walked around the houses, played billiards; visitors came, and later on in the evening people went to the card tables and played a game of L'hombre or whist and usually parted company at 10 p.m. . . .

ANNA HEEGAARD was the source of much speculation and conflicting history. We know that she was the daughter of a freed woman as well as herself free. At one time she owned fifteen slaves, only to give most of them their freedom. She also owned considerable property in Christiansted, inherited from her mother. She was the mistress of at least three other white men before she joined von Scholten in

their long relationship, which was terminated only by the misfortunes of history. At that time the Danes forbade marriage between white and colored, and it was very much the custom of the times for government officials, whose wives stayed behind in the home country, to form other relationships.

We know also that Anna must have had a deep influence on von Scholten and his attitude and relationship to her people. He asked the home government many times to consider giving the slaves their freedom. The Danish government did consider this, but delayed it because of uncertain economic conditions and because many planters protested against it.

The Governor-General was always ahead of the home government. He was the first to give Negroes good government jobs, and twice a week he held brilliant receptions to which both Negro and white residents were invited.

REBELLION AND FREEDOM.   Time was running out, and the stage was set for rebellion with the characters onstage: a liberal Governor; his free-colored mistress; reactionary or dubious planters; a slow-moving home government; some 5,000 free Negroes, and some 17,000 slaves on St. Croix who wanted their freedom.

By C. E. Taylor

The spark which lit the tinder was a move on the part of Denmark which was intended as a step forward. The Danish King in July of 1847 proclaimed a gradual emancipation program to stretch over twelve years. In this period each baby born was to be free, then all slaves to be free at the end of that time.

The slaves had anticipated full, immediate freedom. They were bitterly provoked. The unrest and the underground tension mounted, although much of the white population seemed unaware of its seriousness.

Late in the night of July 2, 1848, the conch shell-horns began to blow and the estate bells to ring; usually signals of fire. This time they were the rallying call for a freedom march on Frederiksted, led by a young Negro, Buddhoe.

Governor von Scholten was alerted finally and spent the night consulting with his officials in Christiansted until daylight. Conflicting and confusing reports came in, but when it became apparent where the trouble centered, the Governor left in his carriage for Frederiksted.

Frederiksted, meanwhile, was in a turmoil. Reports came in that some estates were burning. The Negroes were demanding full freedom. Von Scholten arrived to confront a still orderly but determined crowd of some 8,000 Negroes who demanded freedom or the burning of the Fort and the estates. The situation was tense and dangerous; once the destruction and rioting began, nothing might stop it.

51

The Governor-General acted decisively. Shortly after his arrival he stepped onto the ramparts of the Fort and read his famous Proclamation of Freedom. It began:

All unfree in the Danish West Indies are from today free.

Von Scholten had long desired and pressed for this freedom, but he was acting on his own in direct contradiction to the King's orders and to the plantation owners' wishes. There were those who later accused him of collusion in the uprising and easy capitulation.

The Negroes dispersed to celebrate, and the Proclamation was ordered printed during the night for distribution. Meanwhile, word came that the Christiansted Negroes were gathering in a threatening manner. Von Scholten rushed back there, to arrive just as real trouble began when a young lieutenant fired on the crowd against orders. The Negroes formed mobs and began the systematic burning and looting of the hated Greathouses and the cane fields. They harmed no whites.

The planters were angry and refused to accept the Freedom Proclamation. Under great pressure, von Scholten turned over his military powers to a group of officials who declared Martial law and threatened to shoot the rioters. Von Scholten, badly shaken and shocked by events, and foreseeing the end of his fight for human rights, resigned and retired a sick man. He is supposed to have had a slight stroke. In any case, his physician advised him to leave for Denmark immediately, where he would also have some hopes of vindicating his action in freeing the slaves.

Von Scholten left on July 14, never to return. His case went to court and he was sentenced to be dismissed from all his duties. Long after the Danish King had confirmed his Freedom Proclamation, von Scholten's appeal to the Danish Supreme Court cleared him unanimously of all blame.

Peter von Scholten died six years after he issued the Proclamation. He never lived to see St. Croix again, nor his beloved Anna Elisabeth. She who shared his love and life for so many years was buried on an estate owned by a relative, not far from the beautiful Bulow's Minde where she died in 1859.

Von Scholten lives on in memory as a man ahead of his

Courtesy "Vore Gamle Tropekolonier"

time, hero of the slaves and of those who held human life and rights above their economic interests. He was a great humanitarian and a great man. He was not the only hero of the slaves; others shared in the fight for emancipation.

By C. E. Taylor

BUDDHOE. During the slave rebellion several other figures emerged as heroes, honored to this day with loving memory in folk legend and song. One of these was Buddhoe, whose actual origins may never be known. His real name was Moses Gottlieb, but history knows him as General Bordeaux or Buddhoe. He was a young, intelligent and handsome Negro, a skilled sugar-boiler at Estate La Grange.

Buddhoe was reputedly a friend of Governor von Scholten's and it was this fact that later made the Governor's critics accuse him of complicity in the revolt for freedom.

When the conch shells blew and the bells rang, the Negroes had left their estates and headed for Frederiksted Fort. Buddhoe led the early morning march, yet he controlled the mob. Legend has it that he wore a colorful uniform, carried a sabre and rode a white stallion. The workers carried their cane cutting "bills" and some had fire brands. Buddhoe forbade burning or plundering and gave orders that no white person was to be killed.

Later in the morning, the Danish Fire Chief, Jacob Gyllich, and Frederik von Scholten who was a brother of the Governor, joined with Buddhoe in helping to control the huge mob which rallied at the Fort demanding freedom and offering to burn the town unless given it.

After the actual Freedom Proclamation was read by the Governor, most of the mob dispersed noisily but peacefully to celebrate. One band of rioters, however, called "The Fleet" began roaming the countryside burning and plundering in the center of the island under the leadership of a man named King.

Buddhoe and Major Gyllich confronted the band at Estate Slob, and in the turmoil Buddhoe saved the Major's life. For days the two men ranged the island telling the Negroes of their freedom, quelling the mobs and appealing for order. By July sixth, the militia had been reinforceed by troops from St. Thomas and Puerto Rico.

MARKET SCENE, St. Croix   Courtesy New York Public Library

It was a matter of time until the officials would arrest Buddhoe. Major Gyllich took him to his home for safekeeping against retaliation from officials or planters. When they did come for him, the Major insisted on riding to Christiansted with him and for a few days shared his prison cell as a protest.

Buddhoe was interrogated for weeks, but staunchly refused to implicate Governor von Scholten in the uprising. The new Governor, sent to investigate the whole situation, decided to deport Buddhoe. Major Gyllich and others gave him money and clothing before he was sent aboard a Danish Man o' War. He was quickly parted from the money and clothing and put in irons. Records show he was put ashore at Trinidad, penniless and with old clothing. It is thought that he moved later to Grenada island and died there — but on St. Croix the belief also persists that he went to the United States.

THE AFTERMATH.   Freedom did not bring with it all the things the Negroes had hoped for, nor all the things the planters had feared. It brought a long series of compromises. Events simmered down, but slowly. Life did not go back to normal and a long period of readjustments began. There were new Labor Regulations drawn up for the freed population and it took several years to work out all the issues.

The Negroes found they had to work as usual if they wanted to eat and take care of their families. The planters found it cost them no more to pay wages and provide housing than it had cost them to support the slaves.

The laborers grumbled because they had to sign on for one year at a time and did not have quitting privileges except on each October first on Contract Day. On this day they could change employers. The terms were the same on all plantations.

Twice the government arranged for the importation of "coolie" labor from India — in 1855 and 1863 — this provided a fresh labor supply under a contract with the Indian government.

A few years later a great fire in Bassin, as Christiansted was still called, destroyed thirty-six dwellings, the Anglican Church in part and a schoolhouse.

As if this weren't enough, the worst year in island history, 1867, was a year of one disaster after another. Yellow fever, smallpox and cholera were raging in St. Thomas and St. Croix had to bar ships from her sister island. A severe hurricane hit here in October. All this was climaxed by the great earthquake in November which came in two severe jolts. The sea receded, leaving its bed quite bare, and then according to an early historian "gathering itself up into one mighty ocean wall it came toppling over in immense rollers, carrying all before it. Schooners, brigs, boats and skiffs were washed ashore . . . at Gallow's Bay, twenty houses were demolished."

Frederiksted inhabitants were shocked to see the U. S. warship "Monongahela" sitting inland about where the market now is. Eventually they dug a basin around her and a canal to the sea and floated her back again!

Calamity followed calamity. Next there were several years of poor crops and at times the island was on the verge of bankruptcy. Then — another terrible hurricane in 1876.

THE LABOR RIOTS. Two years later the frustration of the laborers came to a dramatic climax of riots and burnings. It began quietly enough on October first when new contracts were to be signed. This was a day free from work and the Negroes began to drift into Frederiksted in large numbers. Suddenly in the afternoon the rioting began and the first mob attacked the Fort and was fired upon. An urgent message sent to Christiansted for reinforcements did not arrive

QUEEN MARY   By C. E. Taylor

Queen Mary away ya go burn.
Don' ask me nothin' 'tall
Just give me match and oil
Bassin Jailhouse ata we go burn.

RIOTERS, 1878

there until after midnight. By that time Frederiksted was a river of fire with all of Bay Street burning. The puncheons of rum in the warehouses exploded like cannon. The inferno went on all night and by dawn nearly half of Frederiksted was gone.

The military declared a State of Siege against the bands now roaming the country-side burning and looting estates. It took five days to subdue the rioting, with over one hundred lives lost. Nearly all the estates along Centerline west of Kingshill were burned out. Near Christiansted, Anna's Hope and Work and Rest went up in smoke, but the town itself was left unharmed.

Not only the men were the heroes to the laborers this time. Women too played their part in the action and the most famous was:

QUEEN MARY. The mobs of women and children who lit the rum or kerosene to burn Frederiksted, factories and Greathouses while their men fought the Militia had several leaders. Queen Mary was the imposing head of one mob. A famous old Carasou folk song celebrates the part played by Queen Mary, Queen Agnes, and a third, Queen Matilda, who was known simply as "Bottom Belly."

Later Queen Mary spent some time in the Bassin Jail, and along with the two other Queens was supposedly sent to Denmark for trial and prison. They were returned eventually to St. Croix.

The ferocity of these Cruzan women during this great "fire burn" in which forty-four estates, two schools, a customshouse and police station, a big cane weighing house at Peter's Rest and half of Frederiksted went up in smoke, is still spoken of with awe. Fire was the Negroes' one weapon against any kind of enslavement and it was used with great determination in the fight for freedom and labor rights.

DOWN AGAIN, UP AGAIN. The period after the Labor Riots was another one of adjustment and compromise. The labor regulations were made more liberal, and the tension lessened. Frederiksted was rebuilt with late-Victorian gingerbread charm. In general, however, it was still a period of slow decline. There were a few temporary financial rallies in the closing decades of the 1800's, but the old, grandiose days were gone. Denmark found its islands were a burden.

One factor lay in the growing absentee ownership, with the profits of the good years drained off to England, Denmark or other countries. Planters left in discouragement, putting their estates into the hands of the Scotch and Irish managers, who often managed to acquire title by purchase for unpaid taxes, or assumed ownership by default.

The slow conversion to new methods went on, and the last big effort in this line came when the huge Bethlehem Central Sugar Factory was built in 1904 to serve the entire island.

Great hopes were aroused in the islanders when the United States bought the Danish Virgin Islands in 1917 for $25,000,000 after several earlier negotiations for purchase had failed.

The hopes of the three islands for a fast economic growth were dashed again when the impact of prohibition hit the rum industry. A few islanders turned to rum-running. Again St. Croix, which had many times been a smugglers' paradise under its various owners, survived partly by way of its rum, which still meant the difference between profit and loss.

The depression of the '30's in the States was reflected here with much needed pump-priming, government aid, homesteading programs, the WPA and welfare programs. During these years, the CCC planted thousands of roadside trees including most of the mahoganies and all of the tall old coconuts on Centerline Road.

Some self-government was realized with the adoption of The Organic Act, or Constitution, in 1936, set up by the U.S. Congress. This provided for an appointed Governor and an elected local Senate to serve all three islands.

BAMBOULA

SOME FOLK AND OTHER LORE

A L L through these early centuries the Negroes of St. Croix developed their own customs and their own secret ways of compensating for the hard and sometimes cruel life. There was the joyfulness of music and dance and religion. Superstition often played a large role in adjusting to the environment as it also still did with the white population. Among the most interesting of the superstitions are those involving our local spirits.

JUMBIES.   These supernatural beings were to St. Croix what voodoo was to Haiti and Obeah to Jamaica. No one has ever laid hands on a Jumbie, but they were as prevalent as were New England witches. They fought a losing battle and retreated mostly to a position of respect in folklore, love potions, food beliefs and medicinal lore.

The term carries over in such local botannical names as Jumbie Beads, Jumbie Pepper Bush and Jumbie Cutlass.

Some sixty years ago there stood a huge silk cotton tree at Estate Crequis which bloomed in the low narrow valley where there was a perennial "gut" or watercourse. This tree was a rendezvous over the years for the remaining Jumbie believers. It was thought to contain a supernatural force which made the tree walk at night.

One of the trivial but indicative ways a Virgin Islander still propitiates the spirits is never to admit to feeling "fine." He is always "not too bad" or sometimes "nothing worse."

In Carib times the bush kallaloo was often used, and it is now the word for a dish, with the plant as one of its many ingredients. It is thought to be a love plant with match-making abilities. The "leaf of life" is also useful in getting a spouse. The "lucky nut," the "burning love," and the "crazy love" vine have meanings clear to those in the know. Soursop, by local legend, adds virility, but is also a tranquilizer!

If one scoffs at the influence of Jumbies, one should do so while walking under a ladder on Friday the 13th.

THE WEED WOMEN. The ways of the "old life" on St. Croix are fast disappearing, yet there remains one unusual and functional group, known as the Weedwomen, who still practice their ancient healing arts with herbs, simples and drug plants known locally as "bush."

These island practitioners are nearly all women who have little use for Jumbies or any religious connotation in their work. They simply know the sixty or more medicinal plants; know their usages, dosages, their toxic properties and, we hope, their own limitations. The knowledge has been handed down for centuries, but in view of the present generation's lack of interest, it is soon likely to be lost. Two men of our Department of Agriculture, Dr. A. J. Oakes and Mr. M. P. Morris gathered information for several years on the Weedwomen and their usages of medicinal plants, and incorporated it in an article published in 1958 by the Bulletin of the History of Medicine.

The Weedwoman holds a position of respect and admiration in her community; her work is serious and skillful within its range. Combinations of plants are often used as sedatives and to treat fevers, muscular pains, colds, intestinal disorders, etc. The prescriptions include detailed instructions on the parts of plants used, methods of preparation and dosages, along with dire warnings about their mis-use.

Whether there is a logical, medical basis for such practices is at present a moot question. Many of the plants have been studied and tested chemically, and some are in actual pharmaceutical use. Considering the strange, and wonderful, discoveries of modern medicine, who is to say for sure that the Weedwoman with her ancient lore is behind times, or sometimes ahead. Least of all to object are her

THE WEST INDIAN WEED WOMAN CALYPSO

She had her dress tied up over her waist
And was wriggling down the street
She had on a pair of old slaps on her feet
Just then she started to name the
different weeds
And I really was more than glad
Although I can't remember all
that she called
These are a few she had:

Man tiabba, woman tiabba
Tantan fall back and lemon grass
Ninny root, gully root, granny backbone
Bitter payee, lime leaf and toyo
Coolie bitters, corilah bush
That ah the old time iron weed
Sweet broom, sprout and wild daisies
Sweet fate and even toyo.

She had bitter gomma, portogee bomba
Conga Larua and twelve o'clock broom
Sarsparilla, wild tomato, soursop leaf
And Papa bitch weed,
Wild bush, wild cane, wild leaf,
monkey liver
That's bitterer than wild bay root.
Action stands and even monkey liver
And all the rest you may need.

She had pap bush, elder bush,
black pepper bush
Then soldier, corporal and carpadulla
Fabian leaf, money bush, soldier posely
Pumpkin blossom and even devil doer.
Demon Congo, grass in galore
Physic nut, and lily root
In fact the only bush she didn't have
Was the bush for the everyday soup.

From: Trandalier Jones, "Impressions of
Nutrition Habits in The Virgin Islands."
Nutrition Division, Virgin Islands Dept.
of Health, Bulletin No. 11, 1952

satisfied customers who have celebrated her in a famous local calypso adapted from an old Trinidadian song.

INDIGO AND COTTON. These were once two of the island's staple crops, along with cassava and tobacco. The French tried out indigo plantations, as the blue dye was valuable in Europe until the sea route to India opened new sources. There were two species of the plant on St. Croix.

When the Danes bought St. Croix, the first Governor to look it over thought it had a large enough area for 1,000 cotton plantations in addition to an equal number for sugar. This optimistic figure was never reached but the Oxholm map published in 1794 after nearly ten years of surveying showed approximately 40 cotton estates, all east or south of Christiansted. Export figures show that an average of 93,000 lbs. of cotton was shipped out for several years around 1780; had gone down to 79,000 lbs. in the early 1790's, and slipped to 11,000 lbs. after the turn of the century. From this time on cotton became less important and these estates converted mostly to cattle farms. The last cotton ginnery in Christiansted didn't close down until the 1920's, however, and the one at Estate Longford closed about the same time.

Today in the spring and summer the wild cotton still can be seen with its pods bursting over the East End hills.

FLORA AND FAUNA. On St. Croix there is a great deal of flora and not too much fauna except for Cruzan dogs, no two of which seem

exactly alike. The fauna includes our worst pest, the mongoose. It also includes our delightful small white-tailed deer; a few iguana; various types of small lizards; cave bats, fish bats and insect bats; tree rats and the usual ship rats — and, naturally, the persistent mouse.

The mongoose dealt effectively with the two kinds of harmless snakes which once were here, while it did not eradicate the cane field rats it was brought in to destroy.

Among our birds are seven kinds of heron and egrets, five kinds of pigeons and doves, the grey kingbird (chincery), the pearly-eyed thrasher or thrush, the grass quit, two kinds of hummingbirds, and the lovely little banana quit (yellow-breast or sugar bird). There is also the Ani, or Black Witch, which local legend says can be made to talk. Add the graceful terns, the spectacular dive-bombing Pelicans and the majestic Man o' War birds. In the winter a dozen or so northern birds, mostly warblers, join the human tourists here. A determined bird-watcher can keep busy identifying a surprising variety, and there is a local checklist for sale, which helps.

When it comes to flora, every visitor soon learns the ubiquitous hibiscus, oleander, bougainvilla, cacti and aloes. From there on it takes a reference book to learn St. Croix's myriad plant life found in the cultivated garden.

Consider instead some of the native plant life and tree lore. Apples? We have them as-in: pine, belle, maiden, moss, dog, star, sugar, mamee, golden and sweet. We have also the poisonous Manchineel apple which the Indians used to poison their arrows. These little green beach apples made Capt. John White's men ill when they stopped here in 1587 on their way to Virginia.

We have such wonderful flora as Woman's Tongue, nothing nut, catch-and-keep vine, monkey-don't-climb, clashie melashie, poor man's orchid, powder puff, chucu, man jack, lady of the night, cassava, jump-up-and-kiss-me, silk cotton,

cakalaka, diddle doo, sweetsop and soursop, calabash, tamarind and Whitey Mary. The list is endless.

WEST INDIAN CURRENCY. Money in the West Indies was as varied as the many nationalities settling here. The Danish *rigsdaler* (or *rixdaler*), the French *livre,* the Dutch *thaler,* were all good stable money on their own islands.

Since buying, selling and smuggling among all the islands was lively, it was the Spanish or Mexican dollar, the Piece of Eight, which acted as the common denominator for commerce. This famous silver piece was first minted at Mexico City by the Spanish government in 1607. They were issued by the millions until 1821. The coin was divided into four *pesatas* and eight *reales,* and named for the latter. A *real* was worth 12½¢, or one *bit.* Later the United States based its dollar on the Spanish unit; hence our "two bits."

The Mexican monetary system served both the pirate and the commercial world in the Caribbean for hundreds of years until Mexican silver lost its value in 1892. The U.S. dollar had gradually become the leading, stable monetary unit in this hemisphere.

The Danish rigsdaler was rated by the Fifth U.S. Congress in 1799 at 100¢ on the dollar, and when the U.S. bought the islands in 1917, the National Bank of the Danish West Indies kept the right to issue notes until 1934 — these became the only paper legal tender of the U.S. to bear the portrait of a foreign monarch.

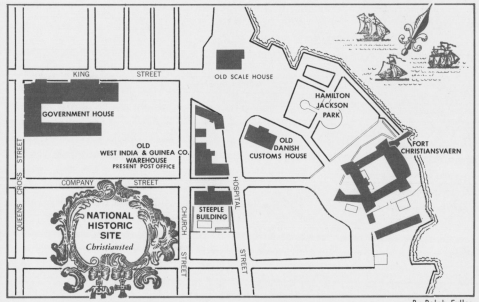

By Ralph Fuller

CHRISTIANSTED HISTORIC SITE

T H E picturesque wharf area of Christiansted is now a National Historic Site under the supervision of the U.S. Park Service, which offers daily walking tours of the area and buildings. Enquire at their office in the old Fort for the schedule.

FORT CHRISTIANSVAERN. A typical example of 17th and 18th century military architecture built by the Danes. Finished in 1749, it was a garrison for the army and later a police station. Many changes have been made: a Commandant's quarters, a powder magazine, a stable and other parts added.

GOVERNMENT HOUSE. Originally a merchant's house, it was bought in 1771 by the government for headquarters, and for living quarters of the Governor-General. Two years later it was remodeled and again in the 1818-20 period. At this time an adjoining house on the side street was bought and added. There were extensive repairs in 1864 and expensive furnishings bought for it. A fire in 1936

STEEPLE BUILDING   By Fritz Henle

damaged it badly, and a new third story was added for living quarters . . . The Danish government has been most generous in helping refurnish it in the original elegant style.

THE STEEPLE BUILDING. One of Christiansted's most historic landmarks, this beautiful old building was put up in 1750-53 as the Lutheran or State Church; with the steeple added in the 1790's. By 1831 the Lutherans gave up the building as in bad condition, and it became at various times a military bakery and storehouse with many structural changes, as well as a hospital at one time. It was closed for many years. After research and years of authentic restoration work under the direction of architect Fred Gjessing and historian Herbert Olsen, it opened its doors again early in 1964 as a museum for the National Historic Site under the Park Service.

THE LIBRARY BUILDING. This graceful two story building was at first only one story when completed in 1751 to be a Customs House. It was modified and the second story added in 1828-30. It was later used as a Post Office.

THE OLD SCALE HOUSE. This is the building that now houses the V.I. Tourist Bureau downstairs; the Harbormaster's office and the Chamber of Commerce above. It was a weighing station for the Customs House. The old scales are still there, where the out-going bales of cotton, hogsheads of sugar and puncheons of rum were weighed, as well as all the exotic in-coming cargo.

THE POST-OFFICE BUILDING. This rambling pink structure with its inner courtyard was completed in 1746-49 to serve as the big warehouse for the original Danish West India and Guinea Company which first colonized the island.

GOVERNMENT HOUSE

By Fritz Henle

THE ST. CROIX LANDMARKS SOCIETY

THE LANDMARKS SOCIETY is an island organization with many long-range plans for restoration and preservation projects. First among these is the complete restoration of Whim windmill into running order. When the mill is restored, island visitors and residents alike will be able to see exactly how such a mill looked and worked in the late 1700's.

Currently the Society is also establishing a new Plantation Museum wing in the old stone buildings back of the Whim Greathouse. Here is told the story of sugar and rum in the working life of an old plantation. Nearby, it is planned to restore an old cookhouse and a sugar boiling house.

These are just some of the many projects the Society has in mind for the future of St. Croix. Since it is a non-profit organization dependent upon membership fees, a yearly grant from the Virgin Islands Education Department, donations and such money-raising projects as its annual House Tours in the Spring, many of its plans must materialize slowly.

Meanwhile, the Society also acts to help in planning for orderly future development on the island in keeping with the present historic atmosphere. The Society has made a never-ending watchdog effort against such encroachments as billboards on our highways, large signs in the towns, neon signs, ugly telephone poles alongside Government House and opposition to highway construction which would endanger the appearance of the harbor and Historic Site.

The history of the Society shows many accomplishments. It is an amalgamation

By Fritz Henle

WHIM GREATHOUSE

of two former groups: The St. Croix Museum and the Landmarks League, which joined forces in January, 1963. During the past sixteen years of their existence, the two groups were responsible for the following:

Establishment of the National Historic Site and zoned area around the wharf at Christiansted, now under the direction of the U.S. Park Service.

Establishment of a Museum in the Christiansted Library Building, with exceptional displays of Carib and Arawak material, and interesting exhibits of local Danish history. (Now in Steeple Building).

Transfer of the historic Steeple Building to the Park Service, which has restored it with care, to become a Museum encompassing some of the material from the old museum. Transfer also to the Park Service of the Folmer Anderson Collection of Carib and Arawak artifacts.

The restoration of the Whim Greathouse, one of the most fascinating showplaces of St. Croix open to the public.

Conducting annual House Tours each February and March which include some eight mornings of tours through restored plantation mansions, and other famous old homes, plus many beautiful new tropical homes.

Acquiring reproductions of the original mirrors and chandeliers for Government House from Denmark where the originals are now in one of the Royal Palaces. Acquiring also the portrait of Alexander Hamilton and a reproduction of a portrait of King Frederik VII of Denmark, both of which now hang in Government House.

DANISH
SENTRY
BOX

The reproduction of an authentic Danish Sentry Box now set up outside Government House.

Re-doing the old Danish street signs on local mahogany.

An "Award of Merit" from the American Association of State and Local History was given the Society for "unusual and highly meritorious work." The Society is also affiliated with the National Historic Trust.

The Landmarks Society, as offspring of the two parent organizations with all their accomplishments, maintains an unceasing effort toward the preservation of St. Croix's unique assets and history. It has succeeded so far through the efforts of many interested, generous and dedicated persons, both here and in the United States. The members are proud of what has been done, and welcome all who wish to join them in their plans for the future.

FREDERIKSTED WATERFRONT   By Toby Schoyer

APPENDIX

Acknowledgements

THE author is greatly indebted to many groups and persons for assistance or previous research, but in particular to all the Trustees of The Landmarks Society; the Public Libraries of St. Croix, St. Thomas and the New York City Library's Schomberg Collection of Negro History & Literature; and to Mr. Ralph Fuller and Mr. Cyril Marshall, current and former Directors of the Landmarks Society.

Also to Dr. Richard Bond, Director of the U.S. Department of Agriculture in St. Croix and members of his staff; to Mr. John Fitter, Mr. Fritz Henle, Miss Val Jacobs, Mrs. Amy Jones, Mr. Eric Lawaetz, Mr. Walter Lewisohn, Mr. Harry Neumann, Historian Herbert Olsen of the U.S. Park Service, Miss Verna Penn, Mrs. Frances Rice, Mr. George Seaman, Mr. Toby Schoyer, Mr. Gordon Skeoch, Mr. Norman Skeoch, Mr. George van Riper, Mrs. Hope Whitman and Mr. Kirk Wilkinson.

By Special Permission

By permission of Alfred A. Knopf Publishing Co., New York, information on slavery, historical periods, trade, the sugar cane plant and its history, taken from "Caribbean, Sea of The New World" by Germán Arciniégas, 1946, Transl. Harriet de Onís.

By permission of Macmillan & Co. Ltd., London, for information on the rum trade with North America, on sugar plantations and history taken from "A Short History of The West Indies" by J. H. Parry & P. M. Sherlock.

By permission of copyright owner, G. P. Putnams' Sons, N. Y., information from "Rum, Romance and Rebellion" by Charles W. Taussig, pub. Minton, Balch & Co., 1928, used in Rum & Revolution, Ye Olde Rum Drinks, Rum-ination, and George Washington's Bar Bill.

By permission of Longmans, Green & Co. Ltd., England, extracts from "Sources of West In-

dian History" by F. R. Augier and Shirley C. Gordon, used in Rum & Revolution, Fortune or Folly and Highlights of History.

By permission of Pomona College, Claremont, Calif., material from Dr. Waldemar Westergaard's "The Danish West Indies Under Company Rule," MacMillan Co., N. Y., 1916.

By permission of the publisher, Pocket Books, Inc., N. Y. and the publisher's agent, Scott Meredith Literary Agency, Inc., material from "The Basic Ideas of Alexander Hamilton", Ed. Richard B. Morris. 1957.

By permission of Harper & Row, N. Y., material used from "The Mind of Alexander Hamilton" edited by Saul K. Padover, 1958.

"The West Indian Weedwomen of the United States" by Dr. A. J. Oakes and M. P. Morris, used by permission of the Bulletin of The History of Medicine, Johns Hopkins Press, Baltimore, Md.

By special permission of the present copyright owner of "Vore Gamle Tropekolonier," Vol. II, Hassing Forlag of Copenhagen, Denmark, sixteen illustrations have been reproduced.

Use of the pirate flag illustration in the W. I. Currency section is by courtesy of Random House, N. Y., from "The Scourge Of The Indies" by Maurice Besson.

By permission of Longmans, Green & Co. Ltd., England, material was used from "A West Indian Fortune" by Richard Pares.

A Suggested Reading List

FLORA

"A Guide to Tropical & Semi-Tropical Flora." Loraine E. Buck & Richard C. Tongg. Charles Tuttle & Co., Rutland, Vermont, 1960.

"Dictionary of Trees". Great Outdoors Association, St. Petersburg, Florida, 1952.

"Dooryard Supermarket In The Tropics and Sub-Tropics." Ann M. Perry, Ft. Lauderdale, Florida, Tropical Works. 1960.

"Exotica", Julius Roehrs Company, Rutherford, New Jersey. 1959.

"Flowering Plants From Cuban Gardens", Criterion Books, N. Y. 1952.

"Flowering Trees of the Caribbean", Bernard & Harriet Pertshik, Rhinehart & Co. 1951.

"Poisonous & Injurious Plants of The U.S. Virgin Islands," A. J. Oakes & James C. Butcher, Misc. Publication # 882, Agricultural Research Serv. U.S. Dept. of Agriculture.

"Observers' Book of Cacti," S. H. Scott, Frederick Warne & Co., London. 1957.

"Tropical Blossoms of the Caribbean," Dorothy & Bob Hargreaves, Portland, Oregon. 1960.

"Tropical Planting & Gardening," Nixon Smiley, Univeristy of Miami Press, Coral Gables, Florida. 1960.

"Tropical Planting & Gardening," H. F. Macmillan, Macmillan & Co. Ltd., London. 1952.

"Tropical Plants & Their Cultivation," L. Bruggeman, Viking Press, New York. 1957.

FAUNA

"Mammals, Reptiles & Amphibians of The Virgin Islands," George A. Seaman, Fish & Wildlife Service, U.S. Virgin Is.

BIRDS

"Checklist of Birds of the Virgin Islands," George A. Seaman, Fish & Wildlife Service, U.S. Virgin Is.

"Field Guide of Birds of the West Indies," James Bond, Macmillan Company, N. Y. 1947.

SHELLS

"American Seashells," R. Tucker Abbott, D. Van Nostrand Co. Inc., Princeton, N. J. 1954.
(In paperback: "How To Know The American Marine Shells," Abbott. Signet Key Book, N. Y. 1961.)

"A Dictionary of Shells," Great Outdoor Association, St. Petersburg, Florida. 1954.

"A Field Guide To The Shells," Percy A.

Morris, Houghton Mifflin Co., Boston. 1947.

"Caribbean Seashells," Germane L. Warnake & R. Tucker Abbott, Livingston Publishing Co., Narbeth, Pa. 1961.

"Checklist of the Marine Shells of St. Croix," G. W. Nowell-Eusticke, St. Croix. 1959.

"Handbook For Shell Collectors," Walter Freeman Webb, Lee Publications, Wellesley Hills, Mass. 1960.

"Shells, Pleasures & Treasures," Roderick Cameron, G. P. Putnam's Sons, N. Y. 1961.

FISH

"A Dictionary of Fish," Great Outdoors Association, St. Petersburg, Florida.

"The Edge of The Sea," 1954. "The Sea Around Us," 1959. Rachel Carson, Mentor Paperback, N. Y.

BIBLIOGRAPHY

Andersen, Folmer, "Notes On St. Croix," St. Croix Museum Commission. 1954.

Arciniégas Germán, "Caribbean, Sea of The New World," Translated by Harriet de Onís, Alfred A. Knopf, N. Y. 1946.

Aspinall, Algernon E., "West Indian Tales of Old," Duckworth & Co., London. 1912.

Atherton, Gertrude, "A Few of Hamilton's Letters," Macmillan, N. Y. 1903.

Augier, F. R. & Gordon, Shirley P., "Sources of West Indian History," Longmans, Green & Co., London. 1962.

Besson, Maurice, "The Scourge Of The Indies," Random House, N. Y. 1929.

Christensen, Carlo, "Peter von Scholten," Gadgaard Nielsens Bogtrykkeri; Lemvig. Denmark. 1955.

du Tertre, "Histoire Generale des Isles St. Christopher, Guadaloupe, etc." 4 vol. 1667.

Edwards, Bryan, "History, Civil & Commercial, of The British Colonies of the West Indies," London. 1807.

Government of Denmark & Government of Danish Virgin Islands, Miscellaneous Bulletins, Ordinances, and Production Booklets.

Gurney, Joseph John, "Familiar Letters To Henry Clay of Kentucky, Describing a Winter In The West Indies," N. Y. 1840.

Hearn, Lafcadio, "Two Years In The French West Indies," Harper & Bros., N. Y. 1890.

Jane, Cecil, Translator, "The Journal of Christopher Columbus," Clarkson N. Potter, Inc., N. Y. 1960.

Jones, Trandalier, "Impressions of Nutrition Habits in The Virgin Islands," Virgin

Islands Dept. of Health. 1952.

Knox, John P., "A Historical Account of St. Thomas," Charles Scribner, N. Y. 1852.

Labat, Pere Jean-Baptiste, "Voyage aux Iles Francaise de l'Isles Amerique," 8 vol., Paris. 1722.

Ledru, Andre-Pierre, "Ref. Voyage A Teneriffe, Sainte Thomas, Sainte Croix et Porto Rico," Paris. 1810.

McGuires "Geographical Dictionary of The West Indies," U.S. Coast & Geodetic Survey. 1925.

Millspaugh, Charles F., "Flora of The Isle of St. Croix," Field Museum Pub., Chicago. 1902.

Morris, Richard E., Editor, "The Basic Ideas of Alexander Hamilton," Pocket Library. 1957.

New York State Education Dept., "Alexander Hamilton, New Yorker," Albany, N. Y. 1957.

Oakes, Dr. A. J. & Morris, M. P., "The West Indian Weedwomen of The United States Virgin Islands," Bulletin History of Medicine. 1958.

Oviedo y Valdes, "La Hystoria General de las Indies," Spain. 1547.

Padover, Saul K., Editor, "The Mind of Alexander Hamilton," Harper & Bros. 1958.

Pares, Richard, "A West Indian Fortune," Longmans, Green & Co., Eng 1960.

Parry, J. H. & Sherlock, P. M., "A Short History of The West Indies," Macmillan & Co., London. 1960.

"Pocket Almanac For St. Croix," St. Croix. 1863.

Rodney, Admiral (Lord), "Letters Relative To Capture of St. Eustatius, 1781," Pub. John Fielding, London. 1784.

Seaman, George A., "Mammals, Reptiles & Amphibians of The Virgin Islands," Brodhurst Printery, St. Croix.

Smith, James, "The Winter of 1840 in St. Croix," New York. 1840.

"St. Croxian Pocket Companion," Copenhagen. 1780.

Taylor, Dr. Charles Edwin, "An Island Of The Sea," 1895.
"Leaflets From The Danish West Indies," 1887.
"Woodcuts," St. Thomas Public Library. 1938.

Taussig, Charles William, "Rum, Romance & Rebellion," Minton, Balch & Co., N. Y. 1928.

U.S. Park Service, "St. Croix Historical Reports."

Van Riper, George (with Fritz Henle), "St. Croix, Virgin Islands," N. Y. 1952.

"Vore Gamle Tropekolonier," Vol. II, (Johannes Brondsted, Ed.), Hassing Forlag, Copenhagen, Denmark. 1953.

Westergaard, Waldemar C., "The Danish West Indies Under Company Rule," MacMillan Co., N. Y. 1917.

Wolff, Alfred R., "The Windmill As A Prime Mover," New York. 1890.

ST. CROIX LANDMARKS SOCIETY
Box 242, Christiansted,
St. Croix, U.S. Virgin Islands

Annual Membership, per person $10

Contributing $25 to $100

Donor $500

Life $1,000